D1237745

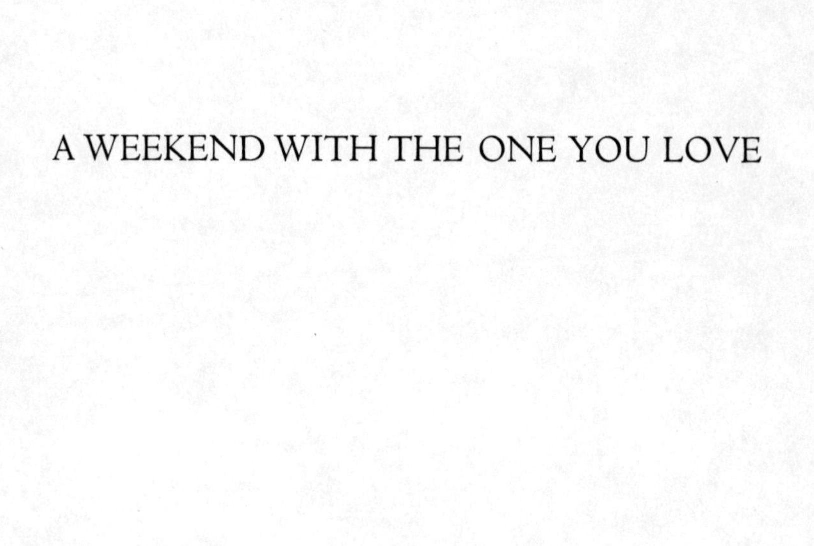

A WEEKEND WITH THE ONE YOU LOVE

A DO-IT-YOURSELF MARRIAGE RETREAT

ART HUNT

MULTNOMAH BOOKS SISTERS, OREGON

A WEEKEND WITH THE ONE YOU LOVE

published by Multnomah Books
a part of the Questar publishing family

Editor: Lisa Baba Lauffer
Copyeditor: Patti Leach
Cover photo: J. Jämsen/Natural Selection
Cover design: Kevin Keller
Interior design: Ellen Cummings

Printed in the United States of America

For information:
QUESTAR PUBLISHERS, INC.
POST OFFICE BOX 1720
SISTERS, OREGON 97759

ISBN 1-56865-361-1

This book is warmly and affectionately

dedicated to my wife.

What a loving partner you are, Naomi.

This book couldn't have happened without

your support and encouragement.

You are God's best and richest gift to me.

Contents

Acknowledgements

How thankful I am to the many people whom God provided to help make this project as good as it could be.

I'm grateful first to Questar's team for partnering with me to make this book possible. Melody Carlson first suggested the concept for the book. Thanks, Melody—it was a great idea! Dan Benson oversaw the publishing process and was a constant encouragement. Thanks, Dan, for your sensitivity, your know-how, and your commitment to this book. Much credit also goes to Lisa Lauffer for editing this project. Thanks, Lisa—you were great to work with. Thanks as well to Don Jacobson, the publisher of Questar. Thanks, Don, for giving me a voice and an opportunity to help couples.

The focus group from Lighthouse Christian Center provided a magical evening and much food for thought. These couples made a real contribution to this book: Angus and Connie McDonald, Jeff and Colleen Smith, Brad and Jennifer Tebbutt, and Larry and Janet Dill. Thanks, friends!

Three couples field-tested this material for a weekend away and gave me valuable feedback: Steve and Karilynn Minor, Angus and Connie McDonald, and Jeff and Colleen Smith. Your comments were a great help—thanks so much.

Thanks to my friend Dave Boyer. His love for enchanting weekends and romantic getaways resulted in many practical suggestions about possible destinations. Thanks, Dave, for your supportive friendship during the writing of this book.

I give all glory and honor to my Lord for any good that comes of this project. He gave me the strength, the ideas, and the time. He was my companion as I wrote in those early morning hours and encouraged me to dream dreams that would bring Him glory. Thank You, Lord!

Introduction

Many books offer *information* about the marriage relationship. I hope for something more from *A Weekend With the One You Love.* I designed this book for *transformation*, actual change in the lives of those who read it. These changes may be small or large—it doesn't matter—whatever the degree of change, I hope this book will help you progress along your marital journey. Couples who deepen their marriage relationships consistently, year after year, do so by making opportunities to better their marriages. This book provides you with such an opportunity.

I've divided this book into four sections. Part One, "What a Difference a Weekend Can Make!" will help you understand the importance of creating a context for marriage enrichment and will give you ideas for planning your own weekend away. Part Two, "Foundations for Marriage Enrichment" consists of four chapters, each outlining a key area of the marriage relationship. If you'd like a weekend away to discuss the basic elements of your marriage, I'd suggest that you plan time during your weekend to read each of these chapters and do the exercises provided. If you'd like to pursue specific issues such as your emotional bond, your sexual relationship, or your financial situation, then plan time to read one or both chapters in Part Three, "Going Even Deeper." Finally, Part Four, "Marriage Enrichment for Life" offers suggestions for continuing your marital enrichment beyond your weekend away. After investing a weekend in growing closer to each other, you'll want to determine ways to continue nurturing your relationship.

I've primarily designed this book as an enrichment tool for

you to use during a weekend away with each other. However, you don't need to plan a getaway to benefit from this book. You could also use this book at home. You might plan six sessions together over several weeks, reading the chapters in Parts Two and Three one at a time and completing the exercises as you go. While you won't be relaxing at a luxury resort, you'll still enrich your marriage!

Regardless of which method you choose, I know that the material in this book can help you move closer together as a couple. As you read this book and complete the exercises, I'm praying that God will help you experience a vital renewal in your relationship, enriching and strengthening your marriage.

Art Hunt

PART ONE

What a Difference a Weekend Can Make!

CHAPTER ONE

What a Difference a Weekend Can Make!

Have you ever wondered why certain couples experience great marriage relationships? Have you ever observed a husband and wife who share a deep love and emotional bond, wishing you could foster that same devotion in your marriage?

In the first few years of my marriage, I remember watching such couples and thinking, "I want to be like that twenty years from now. I'm going to learn the secrets of a successful marriage." What I noticed then and have observed since is that successful couples assign top priority to their marriage relationships. Part of fulfilling that priority is creating and sharing memorable times away. Special getaways merge with other positives in a marriage, slowly weaving a tapestry of committed love between partners. As spouses continue to foster such positive habits year after year, the fabric of the marriage relationship is enhanced and enriched.

Your marriage can grow, too, as you work to improve your relationship by creating a marriage-enrichment weekend for yourselves. This book can help you along. If you'll travel the road suggested in this book, I know that you'll experience growth in your marriage, and your relationship will progress to the next level.

Can a do-it-yourself marriage-enrichment weekend *really* make a difference? Absolutely! Several couples recently enjoyed their own getaways using the material contained in this book. They were couples just like you who wanted to make their good marriages even better. I want to tell you three of their stories. If you're wondering whether *A Weekend With the One You Love* can make a difference in your marriage, listen to what these couples have to say. Discover with them what a difference a weekend can make!

A Needed Focus

Angus and Connie McDonald have been married for twenty-two years. The mother of four children, Connie is the quintessential mom—nurturing, compassionate, patient. Angus is a gentle man with a sense of humor that delights his friends. He works as a manager at a large Seattle tent-and-awning company.

For their weekend away, Connie and Angus traveled by ferryboat to a wonderful bed and breakfast inn on Bainbridge Island. The next day they ferried to Victoria, British Columbia, visited the Butchart Gardens, and enjoyed a nice dinner. Along the way, they discussed the material in this book. Listen to Connie and Angus talk about their weekend together:

> Connie: "One thing really touched me about our time away. We've gone through ups and downs and hard times in life. Not so much in our marriage, but they affect your marriage. During some of those times, we've agreed to get away together soon. Then there was no way that it could work out. But here was a time that it worked out. It really felt as if the Lord was restoring us throughout our time away and replenishing our marriage."

Angus: "I felt the same way. We had a good time, but it was also productive for our relationship. Taking the book along made us focus. It made us remember that our marriage has a life that must be nourished. We've gone away and had fun before, but this time we went to focus on our marriage. It made a difference."

Connie: "In one of the exercises we were asked to remember and discuss meaningful memories we've had as a couple. Yes, it was warm and fuzzy—nothing wrong with that—but it also helped us feel good about our marriage as a whole. When you go through the stressful times, you need to remember that a lot of good has happened, too. There are people who talk only about the stress in their lives, rather than the good times. Our discussion together felt like a deposit in my emotional bank."

Angus: "The chapter on commitment was great. I thought it was so beneficial to refresh our vows and to be reminded of what the marriage commitment means. I liked the section on feelings, too. I always have this paradox, trying to figure out how I'm really feeling and then whether to express it to Connie. This time away reminded me how much Connie wants and needs and appreciates my decision to share my feelings."

Connie: "The materials were a real resource in helping us center in on the relationship."

Angus: "We've been on group marriage-enrichment retreats before. What stands out about this do-it-yourself retreat is that since we were alone, we could totally focus on each other. We could talk for as long as we wanted."

Angus and Connie at first felt a little guilty about taking time and money to focus solely on each other. But their do-it-yourself marriage retreat gave them the time they needed to center on their marriage, and they discovered the importance of investing such precious resources—time and money—in their relationship. Did you sense the warmth they generated during their time together? Connie and Angus returned from their retreat more excited than ever about their marriage. Can a do-it-yourself marriage-enrichment retreat make a difference? You bet!

An Important Discovery

Steve and Karilynn Minor have been married for seven months. They own and run a coffee shop near Pacific Lutheran University in Tacoma, Washington. Karilynn is a tall, dark beauty in her late twenties. At thirty years old, Steve possesses a casual style and ready smile that makes others feel comfortable around him. Steve and Karilynn are both friendly and outgoing—if you met this couple, you'd like them immediately.

Steve and Karilynn planned a camping trip for their marriage- enrichment weekend. But, unbeknown to Karilynn, Steve found a reasonably priced bed and breakfast near their campsite and reserved a room. Because neither was particularly thrilled with the idea of camping, Steve knew this little change of plan would set a happy, romantic tone for their time away.

Despite the change in sleeping accommodations, Steve and Karilynn still enjoyed an outdoorsy weekend, rafting down a nearby river, hiking, walking through a local arts fair. Between their various adventures, Steve and Karilynn read the chapters in this book and did the exercises. They found themselves discussing the material throughout the day. Listen to their reactions:

> Karilynn: "I really liked the exercises and discussion questions. They gave you questions to ask that you normally might want to know but wouldn't

think of asking. We found out things that we didn't know about each other."

Steve: "One thing we did was discuss our lack of prayer time together and how to grow spiritually. We've talked about it before. This time we got specific. What time of day, for example. That was the first time that I found out from Karilynn that praying in bed at night is not good for her because she gets sleepy. For me that seemed like a great place since there were no distractions."

Karilynn: "Our conversations opened a lot of doors for us. It seems that people tend to go on marriage-enrichment weekends after they have problems. Doing this weekend together helped us avoid problems."

Steve: "We made a discovery during our time away. Being newlyweds, we haven't encountered the bumps or circumstances that can make a marriage difficult. We don't have a history of going through rough times. Everything is great between us. We went into the weekend with the feeling that we were doing real well. We came out of the weekend though realizing that there was so much *more* potential in our relationship. The material helped us imagine how our relationship could be even better—that's exciting. It definitely enriched what we already had."

Karilynn: "There are always other obligations that will crowd out your time together. I saw that there is real value in making time to spend with each other in a relaxed setting. It's something that can make a difference in the years ahead for us."

Did you hear the discovery that Steve and Karilynn made? Their do-it-yourself marriage-enrichment weekend helped them imagine how their healthy relationship could become even better. What a great lesson to learn at any time in your marriage relationship! The bottom line for Steve and Karilynn: their do-it-yourself marriage-enrichment weekend made a difference in their lives.

Remembering Again

Jeff and Colleen Smith are dear friends of mine. Jeff is kind, quiet, gentle, and thoughtful. Colleen is outgoing, spontaneous, perceptive, and energetic. Married for twenty years, this couple has an extraordinary relationship. In the years I have known them, I have observed a couple thoroughly in love. What's more, they have spent their whole married life working to enrich their relationship. Jeff and Colleen have carved out the time they've needed to enjoy wonderful weekends away, including a number of group marriage-encounter weekends. This is a couple who knows the value of marriage enrichment!

For this particular weekend, Jeff and Colleen went to a Christian campground in the Seattle area. While their accommodations were definitely rustic, they enjoyed the quiet atmosphere and the little stream running behind their cabin (not to mention the lower price tag). They spent their time together going for walks, shopping, browsing at a local bookstore, and enjoying the beautiful setting of the campground.

Listen to this couple's conversation with me about their do-it-yourself marriage weekend:

> Jeff: "The book was flexible and gave us the freedom to plan the weekend in a way that suited us best. That was great."
>
> Colleen: "In a way, the book allowed us to tailor-make the retreat just for us."
>
> Jeff: "The evaluation exercise at the beginning really

helped us use our time well. It helped us to affirm which areas we were strong in and where we might want to concentrate. When we came to the conflict-resolution chapter, my antenna were really up because we both knew this was a growth area for us."

Colleen: "The section that described how men and women typically handle conflict really floored me. It described Jeff and me perfectly. Knowing how men and women might typically be different helped me to release Jeff in how he processes conflict."

Jeff: "We have a 'blame' problem, so our conflict resolution has not been as good as it could be. On the other hand, we are totally committed to each other so things eventually get handled. It's like we're going over this really rough road every day to get to our house. If we could just pave the road somehow, it would be so much easier! The chapter on conflict resolution really did help us develop some skills to make the road smoother. I gained new insight about the subject. Since we've been on many marriage retreats, that's saying something!"

Colleen: "The exercise at the end of the spiritual-oneness chapter was also excellent. The questions were thought-provoking and helped us to discuss the concepts. The examples were so real."

Jeff: "Really, each chapter gave us something concrete to hold on to. There were examples that helped us relate the concept to *our* situation. Many times we underlined something and then went back through the material to discuss it."

Colleen: "At the beginning of our marriage, we took a marriage class, and we heard some couples say, 'We haven't been away together in twenty years.' We agreed that we didn't want that to happen to us. Our goal has been to grow together all of our married life. This material helped us meet that goal."

Jeff: "One last thing. When we were asked to rewrite our wedding vows, all of a sudden it took me back to my wedding day; how special it was to say my vows to Colleen. During this exercise, I was imagining being there at the altar and watching her come down the aisle. At that moment, my whole world was Colleen. I didn't see anyone else in the church except her. That moment of looking back was worth the weekend, remembering again and affirming our vows."

Jeff and Colleen have spent twenty years creating opportunities for marital growth. On this quiet weekend away, they remembered again the incredible worth of their marriage relationship. They were challenged to grow closer and send marital roots down just a littler deeper.

You're Next!

You, too, can experience what these couples experienced! Whatever your age, location, or family structure, you can spend a weekend together experiencing the warmth of marital growth. You can combine your favorite activities with the additional focus of marriage enrichment provided in this book. You'll return from your time together feeling closer, more in love, and eager for the next time away.

This book is an invitation to spend your valuable time on something invaluable—your marriage relationship! It's a challenge to take the marital relationship you have now and make it even better. And it's an opportunity to create time for each other, to use that time to grow and to just have fun with each other! Such an opportunity is too precious to miss.

The next two chapters will help prepare you for your weekend away. Read the chapters together and do the exercises at the end of each chapter. Then prepare for your time away. As you prepare, remember that this is go-at-your-own-pace marriage enrichment! Make choices along the way to do as much or as little as you'd like.

Come on—you're next! Join the couples in this chapter and experience the warmth, the joy, and the discovery of a do-it-yourself marriage-enrichment party for two!

CHAPTER TWO

Why a Weekend Away?

A Context for Growth

Have you ever experienced a fantastic conversation with your spouse and come away feeling as if something priceless has taken place? Perhaps you shared yourselves freely on an emotional level or set exciting goals together or took care of a problem that was a potential barrier between you. Can you remember the animation, the connection between the two of you after that conversation? More than likely, you came away refreshed, at peace, and more in love than ever. That one conversation made a difference!

Knowing the benefits of such times, you may long for new ways to deepen your relationship together, to renew and refresh your marriage. You know what you need—a day away, a weekend away, any extended time taken together—but with all the other demands on your life, it's so easy to put off. After all, such a trip requires a huge expenditure of one of your most valuable commodities—time.

But the benefits of creating a context for marital growth and enrichment far outweigh the expenditure of time! In the first chapter, you read the positive feedback of three couples who took some time away to concentrate on their marriages. Now, listen to Christian psychologist Neil Warren:

> The value of communication and the intimacy gained...is greatly affected by the context in which it takes place. If that context is characterized by time away from the heavy demands of your routine lives, allowing you to relax and tap into the peaceful, thoughtful parts of yourselves, then your communication—indeed, your entire marriage—is sure to benefit dramatically.[1]

Marriage enrichment thrives on such times. Extended times together create a *context* to send marital roots down a little further; they offer opportunities to focus exclusively on each other.

In the Song of Songs, the Bible's poetic description of romantic love, one of the lovers speaks these words: "Arise, come, my darling; my beautiful one, come with me" (Song of Songs 2:13). In fact, these words form a theme that continues through the last verse of the book: "Come away, my lover, and be like a gazelle or like a young stag on the spice-laden mountains" (Song of Songs 8:14). The lovers communicate the urgency to go away with each other and to focus on their love for each other.

When I've asked couples for feedback after I've led them through one of my marriage-enrichment retreats, they often say something like this: "You know, your input was great, but having the time to *talk* about what you said was the most helpful. Having the relaxed time away for conversation—that was the greatest. We don't know why we let some of these things slide, but we did. This retreat focused our attention again and helped us to talk about some important issues."

These couples simply needed help in creating the context for marriage enrichment.

When a husband and wife take time away to center exclusively on each other, they provide an opportunity for their relationship to grow. At such a time, the couple doesn't just fit their marital relationship around other activities—they make their marriage the main event.

Listen to what one wife discovered about taking time away:

> I used to believe that Jim wasn't interested in sharing his feelings with me. But when we go away on a trip for a few days, and especially when we get away from that darn phone, he seems to relax and get his mind off of work. Those are the times when he does open up.[2]

One husband spoke to me recently about what getting away with his wife meant to him:

> When you create an extended time together, it's as if you cross over a boundary. It's like crossing the Jordan River and leaving that desert behind and you are in a new place. We get into another level in our relationship. Looking back, we have crossed those borders into new areas of our relationship by having an event away, focusing on one another, being tender for a whole period of time together. It's like crossing over into a new land.

Another wife told me simply, "We can be going twenty different directions, but when we go away, we catch up on things." Her husband responded with these words: "Time away focuses our attention on each other. It fills our emotional tanks because it's not just a minute of focused attention, it's a weekend."

The point: Communication is affected by the context! Certainly, these spouses discovered that marriage enrichment was aided by time away together.

As you read this chapter, you may be aware of your need for fine-tuning in your marriage, for catching up with each other, for creating an emotional oasis for your relationship. On the other hand, you might assume that everything is exactly where it needs to be in your relationship. Please know that even the best marriage relationships benefit from periodic examination. Such examination hones your ability to go deeper with the one you love.

Whichever state you find yourselves in, to promote marriage enrichment, create a context for growth—a relaxing environment that allows you to concentrate on each other and input that helps focus your conversation. You provide the environment; this book provides the input.

Growing Marriages Know Where to Aim

I remember reading about a man who loved to target shoot. He used the local stand of timber for target practice with his hunting rifle. Tree after tree in his rural neighborhood had targets painted on them with his shots in the dead center of a bull's-eye. This man was so accurate that the FBI came out and examined the trees. Finally, the FBI agents asked him, "How do you shoot so accurately?"

"Simple," the man said, "I shoot first, and then paint the target in afterwards!"

Are you identifying the target of marital health and aiming toward it or simply taking your best shot and calling it a bull's-eye wherever it hits? If you don't know where to aim, you surely won't hit the bull's-eye. Unfortunately, marriage is one of the few important callings in one's life for which training is not a prerequisite! Rarely does anyone teach couples where to aim. As a result, many couples enter marriage with only an intuitive sense of how to build a healthy relationship. Some couples enjoy the discovery along the way and manage to build a strong and healthy marriage. Others stumble through, never quite moving in the right direction.

What are the essentials for an enjoyable, successful, and growing marriage? As a pastoral counselor, I have spent the last fifteen years working with couples helping them clarify this very question. Often, couples initially express little knowledge of what it takes for a healthy marriage.

Since the most commonly reported problem areas in marriage are finances, time use, sex, and parenting, many couples think that the essentials of a growing marriage have to do with these areas. If they just make sure these "hot spots" are functioning well, then their marriages will be happy. While this is true to a limited extent, it by no means ensures vital marital relationships. Plenty of couples don't argue about any of these issues but still their relationships flounder.

My ideas about this issue began taking shape informally as I examined my own marriage years ago. (Naomi and I have had a happy and fulfilling relationship for over twenty years.) What, I asked myself, had contributed to such an enjoyable marriage? Was it the trust we had for each other, the friendship that we felt? Was it the time we spent together?

At the time, I developed limited answers to these questions, but not until my professional training in counseling in the early eighties could I quantify my thinking further, boiling down these thoughts to a form that any couple could understand. Many experts in the field of marriage enrichment helped solidify my thinking. As well, I spent many hours observing and talking with couples about their marriages and searching the Bible for God's answers.

Through this process I have formed conclusions about what constitutes the essential elements of a healthy and growing Christian marriage. When both spouses actively pursue these elements within their marriage, these elements act as the four corners of a marital foundation, giving stability to all they build later. These four elements are:

1. a biblical commitment to the marriage relationship;
2. an effective communication system;
3. an effective method of conflict resolution; and
4. a strong spiritual friendship, sometimes called spiritual intimacy or, simply, a Christ-centered marriage.

A healthy, growing marriage requires each of these elements. When these elements operate in a marriage, a couple can adequately and lovingly handle other issues such as finances or time use. These elements give the relationship strength and stability, enabling it to grow and flourish and handle the strains brought to it from other issues.

Each of these elements is the subject of one of four chapters in Part Two, "Foundations for Marriage Enrichment," chapters you can read and discuss as you take your own marriage-enrichment retreat.

Why Take a Weekend?

By this time you may think, "We already have these positives operating in our marriage. We're fine." Well, first of all, I suggest that each of you take the marriage inventory at the end of this chapter. The inventory will help you evaluate your marriage at present. Seeing where you are on certain issues may suggest ways in which you can improve.

However, even if all areas look great to you, it is wise to revisit major marital issues periodically. Something that happened to my wife and me a few years ago drove this point home to us. Naomi and I were spending a weekend leading a marriage-enrichment retreat. We were at the incomparable Cannon Beach Conference Center at Cannon Beach, Oregon. The weather was superb, the ocean scenery breathtaking. We had juggled our duties at home and church and made a way to take twenty couples away for a weekend that we hoped would make a difference in their marriages.

I had just taught the first session, and the couples were completing an exercise. I had asked each couple to find a space alone in the large meeting room to spend fifteen or twenty minutes talking through some questions I had prepared. Naomi and I slowly made our way to a window with a beautiful view of the Pacific Ocean and sat down together. I reached for her hand. Neither of us were anxious to start talking. The beauty of the ocean was enough.

I contemplated simply spending our time in silence. After all, I had led marriage retreats for years. We were both thoroughly familiar with the material at hand, and besides, we had discussed this issue many times. To top it off, we were tired. We deserved a break!

But Naomi and I always like to set an example for the couples at our retreats, so we fished out the handout and read the questions. A year before, I had done a similar retreat so the questions were nearly identical to an exercise we had completed then. Naomi began. My job was to actively listen to her, to really hear what she was saying. I concentrated on paraphrasing back to her what I heard her say.

Within a few minutes, something unexpected happened. We hit conversational pay dirt! We were discussing our conflict style as a couple, and Naomi reminded me that when I feel hurt, I tend to withdraw and shut down. She had observed this recently and had let it go, but the exercise had reminded her of it. Since we hadn't considered this part of our marriage for a while, we realized that we needed some further fine-tuning. Suddenly, the exercise took on more importance. We had each other's attention!

We were surprised. After all, we had talked nearly nonstop during the three-hour drive to Cannon Beach that day. In fact, since Naomi and I value conversation in our marriage, we make many opportunities to check in with each other. Yet this item had gone unnoticed, like some inconspicuous stranger in a crowd. We, who had made our marital relationship a priority for so many years, were reminded about the importance of context and communication.

From that time on, Naomi and I decided that every time we asked others to do a communication exercise at a marriage retreat, no matter how many times we had done it before, we'd do it again! Since then, we've had several enriching conversations around topics that we didn't know needed our attention until we talked about them.

Growing Marriages Need Reminders!

One of the important reasons for participating in a do-it-yourself marriage-enrichment weekend is to become aware, and to be reminded again, of factors that make for marital success. After all, repetition is a principle of learning. All of us who labored through fourth grade practicing multiplication tables over and over will agree on the value of repetition! The apostle Peter wrote to New Testament believers, telling them, "I will always *remind* you of these matters, even though you already know them and are firmly grounded in the truth you have received. I think it only right for me to stir up your memory" (2 Peter 1:12–13 GNB, italics mine). One of the tasks of the Holy Spirit is to *remind* believers of the truth (John 14:26). Apparently, believers need reminders to live the truths they've learned. Certainly, this must also apply to truths pertaining to marital stability and success.

Couples may already be "firmly grounded in the truth" of marital success, but they need their memories stirred so that they'll put into practice what they've learned. As couples are reminded of these principles, they benefit by taking opportunities to talk about their relationships in light of these truths. Certain topics tend to come up only when a husband and wife think specifically about their relationship. Are we really listening to each other? Are we sharing ourselves emotionally? Do we accept each other unconditionally? How well are we affirming one another? How well are we handling conflict these days?

Life goes by so quickly, and questions such as these tend to take a back seat to such stirring subjects as "How are we going to get the yard work done this weekend?" True, *any* conversation is great, and in fact, couples in good marriages speak a lot about the day-to-day workings of a home. But talking *about* the marriage relationship is especially important!

When a husband and wife value their relationship, they *make* opportunities to discuss it. Sometimes deep conversation can take place during the high-speed race of life, but couples often need to pause to really evaluate their lives so they can avoid potential problems and foster growth. This can happen *any* time a couple takes time to talk about what's going on in their lives. However, weekend getaways are the perfect environment for couples to remind themselves of vital issues pertaining to their relationships.

Growing Marriages Take Constant Attention

Marriage relationships, like all living things, need constant nourishment in order to flourish and grow. Simply put, marriage relationships need *attention*. It's no good saying that you talked about a particular subject a year ago or that you said, "I love you" to each other a week ago. What has happened *today*?

Marriages are like my house. I live in a two-story home surrounded by evergreen trees. When I clean out the gutters, I think the job should last for a year. But I'm mistaken. Pretty soon, needles and debris choke the downspout again. I think that my front porch light bulb should last for an eternity, and I'm always surprised when it goes out and needs to be replaced. Our furnace has air filters which *should* continue unaffected for ten years or more. Instead, if not cleaned two or three times a year, they simply cease to function.

What's the matter with my house? Nothing! Even superior homes containing good foundations and solid building materials require maintenance. Always, they require attention. In the same way, even superior marriages with great foundations of years together and solid relational skills require maintenance to realize their full, God-given potential.

When you stop and think about it, this need for maintenance is true in every area of life. After all, the downward pull is constant. The science of physics holds to the "second law of thermodynamics." Basically, this law states that every system left to its own devices tends to break down, to move from order to disorder. I have often thought we should postulate the "second law of *relational* dynamics." It would state simply, "Every relationship, left alone, will tend to break down!"

What happens when couples do not give relationships attention? All of us have heard or read stories about marriages which began on some high romantic peak only to end up a few years later in a downward spiral. Anyone who reads "Dear Abby" is aware of the letters from countless spouses who say that their partners just don't treat them like they used to, not giving their relationships the attention that would keep their marriages fresh and growing.

Marriage relationships need attention in order to maintain growth and health. Every relationship, left alone, will tend to break down.

Growing Marriages Take Time

Of course, the maintenance required is costly, demanding the commodity of time. Couples serious about their relationships shouldn't labor under any misconceptions about this. Listen to Mike Mason's assessment:

> Marriage gobbles up unbelievable enormities, scandalous vastnesses, great fantastic globs of pure, priceless, unrecoverable time. It is like the amount of fuel that must be fed into a big, powerful, shiny, eight-cylinder gas guzzler that has to be kept constantly on the road. You cannot leave a marriage sitting in the driveway even for a day.[3]

Mason is right. Marriage is woven together with the fine, silky threads of time. Nothing else will do. Neglect will unravel God's marital tapestry. However, when you infuse time and attention into your marriage, stand back! Your relationship will become strongly knit together. As a result, you'll experience joy and a deepening partnership as a couple.

I want to encourage you to take time to focus on your marriage. On a daily basis, call each other, go out to lunch together, set aside time for evening chats after the kids have been safely tucked in for the night. And take times away together to create a special context for growth that can benefit your marriage.

A few years ago, I entered an extremely busy time in my pastorate. My normal times away with Naomi just got swallowed up, melting away with the demands of our ministry. We managed to keep talking, to have lunches together, to hold it together, but we both felt the pressure. In June of that year, we had a time away scheduled. Naomi and I were praying a few weeks before our weekend came up, and as I prayed, I made this request: "Lord, let this be a wonderful time of listening to each other and growing closer together."

As I thought about it later, I realized that when Naomi and I go away together, we go for one reason: to catch up with each other. Does that mean that we neglect each other between getaways? Absolutely not! We place a high priority on our relationship. But when we take a day or weekend away, we often come back more acutely aware of each other's emotional, psychological, and spiritual state of being.

Of course, when we set aside a weekend for each other, we may do any of a variety of activities. We may read or watch a movie or take walks or shop or...the possibilities are endless! But we understand that we are going away to get current with each other, to gain a fuller understanding of each other and a greater sense of God's presence in our lives and relationship.

That's what we were expecting from our June getaway. When June came and time for our scheduled weekend away arrived, the context for growth was incredibly beneficial. We rode bikes together, played tennis, had a romantic dinner out, prayed together, planned our schedules, and talked and talked and talked. And as we did these things, tension melted away, and our relationship took center stage. We affirmed our marital bond, and a deep feeling of warmth emerged.

Why a weekend away? To give time and attention to the most important relationship in your life. A weekend away allows you to focus your full attention on each other, to return again to quiet talks about forgotten subjects, to spend forty-eight hours extravagantly on each other.

Relationships do not rely wholly on such weekends. After all, life is a daily partnership. I enjoy work days with Naomi, cleaning the garage or painting the hall. With her I wash the dishes, plan dinner parties, pray, talk, take walks. Life together consists of bits of such time that work together to build a relationship.

But romantic getaways can play an important part of a couple's life. Why? Because meaningful conversations usually don't just happen. They require time and attention. Why not make a choice to spend some time on what really matters? Like the couples I discussed in Chapter 1, discover the incredible value of focusing time and attention on each other.

Exercise: Marital Satisfaction Scale

On separate sheets of paper, each of you rate your level of satisfaction with the marriage elements listed below.[4] Zero indicates no satisfaction, five average satisfaction, and ten absolute satisfaction.

1. The depth of our commitment to each other and to our marriage relationship.

0 1 2 3 4 5 6 7 8 9 10

2. The frequency and depth of our communication together.

0 1 2 3 4 5 6 7 8 9 10

3. The way we manage conflict.

0 1 2 3 4 5 6 7 8 9 10

4. Our spiritual partnership, including our prayer life together.

0 1 2 3 4 5 6 7 8 9 10

5. How we express caring behaviors on a daily basis.

0 1 2 3 4 5 6 7 8 9 10

6. How we develop our friendship with each other.

0 1 2 3 4 5 6 7 8 9 10

7. The frequency and enjoyment level of our sexual relationship.

0 1 2 3 4 5 6 7 8 9 10

8. The way we manage our money and divide financial responsibility between us.

0 1 2 3 4 5 6 7 8 9 10

9. Amount and quality of free time and daily involvement together.

0 1 2 3 4 5 6 7 8 9 10

10. The way in which we agree on and implement our parenting skills.

0 1 2 3 4 5 6 7 8 9 10

After you have both circled your answers, find a time to share your responses with each other. Then answer these questions: On a scale of one to ten, how would we rate the quality of our marriage relationship? What does God want to do in our lives as a couple in the coming year? What changes do we need to help us keep growing?

Chapter Three

Preparing for Your Weekend Away

By now, I hope I've convinced you of the incredible value of time away together. In fact, I hope I've done such a good job that you're ready to plan *your* weekend away. If so, keep reading! This chapter will help you prepare.

Your getaway will start the moment you begin planning because you'll anticipate this special time together and put effort toward creating the perfect context for marriage enrichment. As you plan your time away, the three suggestions below may help.

1. Prepare! Prepare! Prepare!

Weekends *must* be scheduled. Opportunities for marriage growth must be created; they don't just happen! This means you'll have the fun of sitting down with each other, calendars in hand, and choosing a time to get away. Don't be discouraged if you must wait three months to go on your trip. You won't believe how quickly that date will arrive! In fact, Naomi and I have noticed how nice it is to anticipate a time away. Just putting it on the calendar is fun!

Many couples like to sit down with their calendars at the beginning of the year and schedule one getaway per quarter. (More and more counselors, even secular counselors and marriage experts, recommend that couples take one night a week for each other, one weekend a quarter, and one week a year. Can you imagine the context for growth this kind of schedule would create?) If you're reading this book in July, however, don't wait until the new year to schedule time away. Find a date some weeks away and make it happen!

After scheduling your weekend, you'll want to decide where to go and make necessary arrangements such as reservations and travel plans. We'll discuss this more in detail in the next section.

Another part of preparation is packing everything you'll need for your time away. One fun way to do this is something Dave and Claudia Arp call the "Get Away Box."[1] This is a place where you can gather everything you'll take on your trip. One of the great things about a Get Away Box is that it helps you anticipate your time away. Thinking ahead to your time together and setting aside special items create warmth and excitement far in advance of the event.

What goes in the Get Away Box? How about that novel you've wanted to read? What about a small gift for each other? Surprises are always nice; each of you purchase something special, wrap it, and put it in the box. Naomi and I also recommend including the following items: sparkling apple cider, champagne glasses, cheese, fancy crackers, delicious chocolate mints, and a votive candle and holder. These items will make a wonderfully romantic snack time on one of your nights away. Music is always nice, too, so don't forget to tuck away a favorite CD or cassette along with a portable player. The Get Away Box might also include any sports equipment you may need. Naomi and I sometimes bring our tennis rackets. Other couples include their golf clubs or jogging shoes. Another suggestion: Take along your calendars. Naomi and I usually bring ours, and we enjoy sitting quietly together and planning time within the next couple of months for each other and for our family. (Look at Appendix A on page 183 for a checklist of things to bring on your getaway.)

One last word. Naomi and I have sometimes planned a time away but have forgotten a crucial item: child care! The moment you agree on a date for your weekend, make it your next step to arrange for the care of your children. Naomi and I use a variety of methods. Occasionally, Naomi's parents have stayed with our kids at our house. At other times, we've parceled out our three children to close friends. However you handle this challenge, don't let your children prevent you from taking your time away. I have known couples who have told me that they haven't been away from their children in fourteen years. Believe me, that's too long!

Get ready to go! Put your date on the calendar and start preparing. As you do, you'll find your marriage enrichment has already begun!

2. Choose Your Destination

Choosing your destination can be a fun part of your preparation; in most parts of the country, you have so many options to pick from. Enjoy yourselves by doing the research necessary for a great weekend.

Before we discuss specifics, let me make one suggestion about a difficult topic: Don't let your financial condition get in the way of spending quality time with each other. Few couples have the financial resources to spend a dream weekend away at a fantasy hotel. In fact, for some even a Motel 6 might be a reach! But even simple accommodations can provide the perfect place and time for relational growth.

One couple I know has taken many getaways over twenty

years. I recently talked with both spouses. They had just come back from a week together in Hawaii, and they told me this:

> You know, the week was great together, but not the best we've ever had. The time we spent camping a few years ago actually was more productive for our relationship. What we've learned over the years is this: It's not where you go, it's what you take with you.

How profound! It's not the location, it's "what you take with you." What any couple takes with them is the desire to grow closer together, an attitude that seeks to go deeper. So as you plan your time away, remember your goal: to create the context for growth, a time of relaxation where you can focus on each other. This can happen in any number of locations.

Having said that, let me give you some information about different places you can stay. *Hotels* derive the bulk of their income from business travelers. This means that hotels will sometimes find creative ways to fill their rooms on weekends. Many major hotels offer some sort of discounted weekend "romance package" to attract weekend customers. Contact two or three hotels you might want to visit, and ask them if they offer any special packages. Some will simply offer a cheaper room; others will offer everything from sparkling cider to roses.

Bed and breakfast inns are rapidly growing in popularity as a weekend getaway for couples. Unlike hotels, "B & Bs" are generally smaller establishments that rent out several rooms and provide breakfast in the morning. Many B & Bs are in lovely historical homes with cozy and intimate atmospheres. Although they don't offer amenities such as health clubs and room service, bed and breakfasts more than make up for these comforts with their quiet settings, lovely environment, and unique locations.

A surprise destination might be just the thing for that extraspecial time away. A few years ago, my friend Jeff Smith really blessed his wife, Colleen, with a special weekend. Jeff planned everything without Colleen even suspecting that they would go away. He made reservations for travel and accommodations. He went shopping and bought everything Colleen would need for the trip, such as clothes, cosmetics, and a hair brush. (He knew that if he took anything from the house, she would figure it out.) Jeff had even cleverly arranged for Colleen to get to the airport without her suspecting anything. When she arrived, Jeff was waiting for her, ready to jet her away to San Francisco for the weekend. Colleen was truly surprised and felt incredibly affirmed and loved. If your spouse enjoys surprises, you could plan an unforgettable surprise weekend with him or her.

On the other hand, you and your spouse may have very little money to work with, but you can still create a context for growth. *Less expensive possibilities* do exist! If money is an issue, you can brainstorm some creative alternatives. Assume it's possible to plan a great weekend together on a low budget, then make it happen! Some couples might decide to drive to a nice location and stay in a motel that's pleasant but not pricey. You can also decide to eat mostly inexpensive foods or bring your food with you. What?! Can couples do a getaway without romantic, twenty-five-dollars-a-plate restaurants? You bet! Romance will come more from *how* you attend to each other during your time away than from the amount of money you spend.

You might choose to go camping. Camping can be great because you'll have few distractions and almost guaranteed quiet. As I mentioned earlier, at least one couple found camping to be one of their most intimate times away. If you're an "outdoorsy" couple, you might find the same to be true.

Other couples might wish to plan just a day away instead of a whole weekend. You'd be surprised how restful even one full day and night away from the routine can be. I remember a time while I attended seminary when Naomi and I definitely needed time away. I went to school fifteen hours a week, studied thirty hours a week, and worked twenty hours a week. On top of that, Naomi ran a day care to help support us. We couldn't afford much, but we did get a whole day away at a nearby motel. We relaxed together, found time to talk and play, and came back more refreshed than when we left.

One other low budget way of spending a weekend together is to prepare to go away...then stay home! Naomi and I have done this on more than one occasion. Farm out your kids, clear your schedule, let people know you're unavailable that weekend, then simply turn off the phone and operate your getaway from home base! When Naomi and I have done this, we've spent our money on a nice dinner and perhaps a movie. We've made excursions during the day, taken walks, and enjoyed ourselves immensely.

Finally, it may be helpful to buy one of the many resources available at your local bookstore that explain the beautiful accommodations close to you. In the Seattle area where I live, we consult *Best Northwest Places* for destinations in Washington and Oregon. Most areas in the country have one or more excellent books that recommend the best hotels, B & Bs, restaurants, and special activities in a given area. Your local bookstore or library can help point you in the right direction.

So choose your destination, and start looking forward to spending time there together!

3. Know What to Expect

Your marital health is the result of *accumulated* positive experiences. The outing you're now planning can be *one* of those great times of fun, relaxation, and directed conversation, but it cannot be everything. Make this getaway the best possible, but don't allow too-high expectations to ruin a great time together.

In fact, set aside time *before* the trip to discuss your expectations of your time together. You'll benefit from knowing what each other has in mind. One of you may be saying, "Hey, this is great. We're just going to go away, relax, and have fun." The other may be thinking, "We're going to be able to do this or that" and have every minute planned. Communicate your individual expectations, take into consideration both of your points of view, then come up with mutually agreeable expectations before you go.

I talked to a couple recently who went to a beautiful bed and breakfast for two days together. They were both tired from months of hard work, so they agreed ahead of time how they would spend their time away. They took three movies along on tape and basically "vegged out" over the weekend. This included Jacuzzi time, good movies, good food, and much warmth and love. While this might not be the ideal schedule for *every* getaway, this couple enjoyed it partly because they had the same expectations for their time away.

So discuss what you expect from your getaway, then do what you can to meet those expectations.

Keep a Balanced Agenda

One of the easiest mistakes to make on a time away is to overplan. Remember, this is marriage enrichment, not a business trip! When you plan your weekend, leave some time open to do whatever hits your fancy at the time. Make sure that you don't make the time so intense that you sabotage your reason for going: to create a relaxed and peaceful environment in which to enjoy each other's company and experience growth.

Emphasize Marriage Enrichment

Of course, I recommend one expectation: Take *A Weekend With the One You Love* along with you and revisit some important relational issues during part of your time away. For optimal results, I suggest that you set aside one-hour or ninety-minute segments, four times over the weekend. Your schedule might look like this:

Friday Night:	Chapter 4, "Committed Love"
Saturday Morning:	Chapter 5, "Skillful Communication"
Saturday Afternoon:	Take the afternoon off and enjoy yourselves!
Saturday Night:	Chapter 6, "Effective Conflict Resolution," or Chapter 8, "Deepening Your Emotional Bond"
Sunday Morning:	Chapter 7, "Vital Spiritual Friendship"

If this sounds like too much to you, simply don't do as many sessions! If you read only two of the chapters and complete two of the exercises over a weekend, you have potentially enriched your marriage. Perhaps you'll need two or three weekends away to work through the book, or you might decide to begin *A Weekend With the One You Love* on a weekend and continue it at home during the weeks that follow. The point is, this is *your* time away. Decide how you'd like to spend it, then have a great time together.

I suggest that you take turns reading each chapter aloud. The longest chapters will take you a maximum of forty-five minutes. (If you want to read the chapters together silently, you have my permission to copy the chapters you will read on your weekend together.) At the end of each chapter, I've included one or more exercises for you to do. I've designed these exercises to help you practically implement the material of the chapter. If you take forty-five minutes to read each chapter and forty-five minutes to do the exercises afterwards, you will have spent a great ninety minutes enriching your marriage!

To help you plan and prepare for your weekend away, I've included an exercise in this chapter, too. I'd encourage you to do it to get yourselves started on a trip that could enrich your marriage!

Exercise: Planning a Time Away

After you read this chapter, find a time to sit down with your calendars and arrange a time away. Have fun discussing the following questions:

1. In the next three months, when is a good time to take a weekend away? Can we agree that this will be our next weekend away together?
2. Keeping our budget in mind, what are our best alternatives for accommodations? Can we agree on one that would interest us both?
3. What kind of weekend do we want: active or quiet? What are our expectations? Can we agree to use *A Weekend With the One You Love* as a way of deepening our time together?

Part Two

Foundations for Marriage Enrichment

CHAPTER FOUR

Foundation 1: Committed Love

Ken and Dora Nickel have been married for forty-five years. They have walked the marital journey together boldly, year in and year out. Flourishing in good times and bad, they have simply joined hands and hearts and *made* their marriage work. Since these two folks happen to be my wife's parents, I've had more than a passing glance at their lives and at their marriage relationship over the years. Believe me, it has been an education!

When Mom heard that I was going to write a book on marital enrichment, she gave me her best shot about marriage before I had even asked her one question! This soft-spoken grandmom was passionate, and what she said was obviously at the heart of her belief about marriage:

> Art, what makes a marriage work is good, old-fashioned commitment. Ken and I are happily married today because we both made a commitment that we never even considered backing out on. That's the secret to a good marriage—commitment.

Experts concur. In his examination of one hundred extremely successful couples, psychologist Neil Warren found that over 90 percent of his respondents attributed their marital success to the centrality of commitment.[1] James Dobson queried 300 couples and found the same thing: Commitment is essential for a healthy relationship.[2]

Christian couples all over the world would nod their heads in agreement. Indeed, when I talk to couples about building healthy and growing marriages, these couples almost always mention commitment as pivotal to making their marriages happy. Couples know instinctively that without commitment, nothing else works in a marriage.

Since you've set aside time for marriage enrichment with each other, I know you're committed to making your marriage work. I hope that the information provided in this chapter will help you make your commitment to each other even stronger.

Marriage Begins With a Promise

This issue of commitment within the marriage relationship is so important that the central element of all marriage ceremonies is a public act of commitment. Couples make promises—vows—to each other! I'm sure you remember the day you made your vows to each other.

Have you ever stopped to think why such vows are emphasized at a marriage ceremony? Why does every marriage relationship need to begin with such promises? Mike Mason writes about this:

> If people were faithful by nature, vows would not be necessary.... But it is because people are not inherently faithful nor honest nor loving that they must stand up and declare that they will be.[3]

Notice Mason's point: We are not *inherently* faithful. So a public act of commitment makes every marriage relationship exclusive; two people announce that nothing will separate them. *Nothing.*

As husband and wife we make these declarations because, though we refuse to believe it on our wedding day, we know that our marriage relationship will not always be easy. Indeed, a newlywed husband and wife soon discover that life brings challenges and transitions and that they must weather these trials as a couple. As they endure these trials, conflict will rear its head, and emotions will flair. During these times of stress, a couple's declaration of commitment to each other keeps the relationship safe and secure. Sometimes that commitment is almost all that the couple has going for them! They can't take the easy way out, because they've said they wouldn't. Instead, they rely on their commitment to, like a lighthouse, lead them through the rocky shoals of conflict and strife.

A Blending of Two Worlds

These challenges and transitions hit us so soon after the marriage ceremony because of the very nature of marriage itself. Mason tells us why: "A marriage is not a joining of two worlds, but an abandoning of two worlds in order that one new one might be formed."[4] Neil Warren puts the same idea in a different way: "The principle challenge of marriage is the weaving together of two complex individual identities and the forming of a corporate identity."[5] That's the immediate challenge: "the two become one" (Genesis 2:24 NEB). Two people must form a new identity, a new oneness. It's an awesome but difficult process that calls for hard work, flexibility, compromise, and ultimately, commitment.

I was amused some years ago to read an article by author Paula Rinehart. She wrote, "My husband and I were fully aware that marriage meant oneness: the only question was, which 'one' of us would our marriage become."[6] Do you see the difficulty this wife articulated? Forming a marital partnership is not an easy business! Marriage requires more from us than we sometimes feel we can give, and thus, the reason for vows of commitment. This process of weaving our worlds together to form a new "corporate identity" pushes us to the limits of ourselves. In fact, at times one or both spouses may feel pushed *beyond* their limits.

Perhaps you remember times in your own marriage that called for extraordinary patience, love, and commitment to keep going. If possible, recall one of those times right now. In that instance, how did your commitment help you endure?

In the times when you stand firmly on your commitment to each other, including the time you just discussed, you more than likely discovered that God empowered you to stay true and to conquer your challenge together. We find that when we *must* make our marriage relationships work, we have to turn to God over and over again for His strength and supernatural love. Our marriage commitment sends us beyond ourselves to the deep reservoir of God's love. As a result, our marriages stay healthy and growing.

Like any other couple, Naomi and I have discovered the importance of committed love over the years. Each of us has made mistakes. We've needed each other's rock-bottom commitment for not only the major struggles we've faced but the minor frustrations and irritations we've experienced as well.

Let me give you an example of a common frustration. Throughout our entire married life I've had a habit that has driven Naomi crazy. I'm a tapper. Don't laugh! When I'm sitting still, I find a pencil or some other object to tap. Or I tap my foot against the table. Or I use my hands to drum a beat. I do these things without even thinking. For over twenty years, I've been driving Naomi out of her mind with my tapping. While this habit may seem small and unimportant, it still takes commitment to endure day in and day out for some twenty years. Thank You, Lord, for Naomi's committed love!

What Is the Marriage Commitment All About?

Let's look at the nature of biblical marriage commitment so that we can gain the renewal and blessings God desires for our marriages. As you read this section, focus on the important aspects of your marriage commitment.

Lifelong Oneness

The essence of the biblical marriage commitment is a pledge of lifelong oneness. "Lifelong" is not hard to understand. Genesis 2:24 clearly indicates that the marriage relationship represents a permanent bond: "For this reason a man will leave his father and mother and be united to his wife, and they will become one flesh." The phrase, "be united to his wife" seems rather routine in the New International Version's translation. The King James Version makes a stronger case: "and shall cleave unto his wife." The Hebrew word for "cleave," *dabaq*, conveys a strong concept. *Dabaq* quite often referred to physical objects sticking to each other, such as bone cleaving to muscle.

In Mark 10: 7–9, Jesus quotes this passage from Genesis and declares, "what God has joined together, let man not separate." "Joined" in the Mark 10 passage means literally to yoke together. God uses the words "cleave" and "joined" to signify the strength of a lifelong commitment.

To what, then, is this lifelong commitment? Oneness. As the Scripture says, "and they will become one flesh" (Genesis 2: 24). This phrase conveys a number of meanings. Certainly the obvious idea is a monogamous sexual relationship. One man for one woman for life. In Matthew where Jesus quotes this verse, He goes on to say: "So they are no longer two, but one" (Matthew 19:6).

God, however, intended this as more than simply a physical union. Hebrew mentality considered the concept of "flesh" as meaning the complete person. To say that a man and woman would become one flesh incorporated the whole of each person: a sexual, psychological, and spiritual union. "The idea of 'one flesh' expresses the complete personal community of one man and one woman as spiritual unity," says Old Testament scholar, Allen Ross.[7] The implication of such a commitment is staggering. What a radical commitment we make to our marriage partners!

Importantly, this oneness is more than a commitment to the marriage; it is a commitment to the person. Seeing oneness as a dual commitment is so important. As one wife told me:

> Stan has always had a deep commitment to me, and I appreciate it. It does feel secure. But I don't want to be with someone just out of obligation. I want an emotional commitment, not just a legal commitment.

This wife made it clear that she highly valued both aspects of the marriage commitment—emotional and legal. Her husband's pledge to her as a person was just as important as his commitment to their marriage. Like the two sides of a coin, each aspect of the one-flesh marriage relationship is incomplete without the other.

Think about your own marriage: Does your commitment reflect more than mere duty? Have you committed yourselves not only to your marriage but to each other as individuals?

Covenant, Not Contract

In the twentieth century, we've viewed marriage as a contractual arrangement. I recently read about a couple who took this idea to its logical conclusion and wrote a marriage contract detailing their expectations for each other, including how many times a week they would have sex! If either failed to live up to the contract, the other could exercise his or her right to break it!

This emphasis on marriage as a contract has tended to place marriage on the same level as other contractual relationships. People enter into contracts with others because of distrust. They want to protect their rights. If an unexpected circumstance arises, they want the right to break free of their contracts. The key word here is "if." If you do something for me, I'll do something for you. If you break your promises, I can break mine.

How differently our Creator sees the marriage relationship! In two places the Old Testament speaks of marriage as a *covenant* relationship. Malachi 2:14 says, "She is your partner, the wife of your marriage covenant." In Proverbs 2:16–17, King Solomon also discusses marriage as a covenant. Christian marriage partners, you haven't just signed a contract; you've entered a covenant!

What is a covenant? It's much more than a contract. A covenant is a solemn agreement that must not be broken. In the Old Testament a covenant carried with it the solemnity of an oath. A covenant was a permanent and unalterable obligation witnessed by God.

In speaking of God's relationship with Israel, the Bible says that "the LORD your God is God; he is the faithful God, keeping his covenant of love to a thousand generations" (Deuteronomy 7:9). In His relationship with Israel and with us, our God demonstrates the kind of faithfulness that He wants His children to emulate. As exemplified by God, the marriage relationship is a covenant of love that helps each spouse remain faithful through good times and bad. The rings you placed on each other's fingers signify that covenant—bright, untarnishable, and enduring.

Have you viewed your marriage as a covenant or a contract?

Unconditional Love

The marriage commitment is an act of the will, not dependent upon feelings, circumstances, or even desire. This commitment finds its roots in the unconditional love that God extends toward His children and that He commands us to give each other.

Romans 5:8 typifies God's unconditional love: "But God demonstrates his own love for us in this: While we were still sinners, Christ died for us." God chose to give to His children without thought of return. In a gracious act of unconditional love, Christ died for us while we were still rejecting Him. When the Scripture says, "Husbands, love your wives" (Ephesians 5:25) and that wives should learn to "love their husbands" (Titus 2:4), God has in mind the same unconditional love.

Committed love is primarily an act of the will, a choice to permanently and unconditionally demonstrate love to another. While the joyous warmth of married love is a powerful benefit of a healthy marriage, that warmth springs *from* unconditional love, not the other way around. Committed love is the cause; the emotion of love is the effect. When couples make a series of decisions to *demonstrate* committed love to their spouses, *feelings* of love tend to follow.

Most pastors and counselors have heard someone say, "I don't love my spouse anymore." Since this person doesn't *feel* love, he or she mistakenly assumes that the relationship is doomed. But nothing could be further from the truth! Whether your spouse is currently lovable or not, unconditional love stays committed! Think about it for a moment. Isn't that the kind of love you experience from God? When you fail, He forgives you; when you don't perform as well as you'd like, He's behind you; when you have periods of doubt, He still loves you. That's unconditional love, and that's what married love is all about.

How can you show each other unconditional love today and in the days to come?

Committed Love Is Active

Committed love also *actively* pursues a growing relationship. Listen to Neil Warren:

> Commitment requires a far more active approach in marriage.... Staying in a marriage can be totally passive; you don't leave, but you don't do anything to make the marriage better.[8]

Think about it. You can commit yourself to your marriage yet remain totally passive about developing the relationship. But committed love is active! Our Father models this kind of love. We see it in John 3:16: "For God so loved the world that he *gave*" (italics mine). Love moved our Father to action—to giving His Son, Jesus.

Dull marriages come alive when couples pursue their marriage vows as an active commitment to growth! Your marriage has so much potential, but you won't realize those positive possibilities unless you decide to serve, listen to, appreciate, and affirm each other. Think of your wedding vows. Many people commit to the following: "to love, to honor, to cherish." Are these words passive? Absolutely not! Instead, they bring to mind pictures of loving acts and loving words. Marriage enrichment leaves no room for passivity.

Family-life specialist Charles Sell makes this point: "Committed love is the essence of marriage—it includes a promise to work together at building 'oneness.'"[9] Building oneness is an activity, something couples *do*. Good marriages don't grow into great marriages unless couples are willing to do what love dictates, to actively build their marriages.

Because you're reading this book, I know that you want enrichment in your marriage relationship. Let me be clear: The responsibility for making your relationship grow lies directly in *your* hands! A growing marriage relationship requires that you make a solid commitment to each other and then make a series of decisions in the years to come to make that commitment active. What choices can you make today and in the weeks to come to keep your love active and alive?

Benefits of Committed Love

When builders construct a large building, they place a stone representing the starting place of the construction. This stone is called the cornerstone. A husband and wife wanting enrichment must always remember that committed love is the cornerstone of their marriage. Without committed love, there will be no growth or health.

Having discussed the importance of commitment, I'd now like to suggest a number of its practical benefits.

Security

You've felt the tension, haven't you, that sometimes accompanies the building of your marriage relationship? The misunderstandings? The temptation to hold a grudge? The plain and simple irritations that come into your life as a couple? Think for a moment about all the decisions you make in just the first year of marriage: who will make the final decision about money management; how you'll split up household chores; who will be responsible for dinner invitations; how you'll handle your sex life. And these just touch the tip of the iceberg of forging your oneness!

When differences arise as you discuss tough issues, one or both spouses can fret about the commitment of the other. As the years mount, fear of abandonment goes even deeper as the prospects of illness or life difficulties present themselves. If you have any doubt about each other's commitment, insecurity develops and hampers the relationship. But when you demonstrate committed love to each other, you constantly reassure each other that you will not leave, emotionally or physically.

Commitment gives a marriage the security it needs to flourish. One wife told me, "My husband's commitment makes me feel much more secure in times of stress. I know he's there. I know we'll work it out." When both partners can relax, knowing that they will not be abandoned, a couple can freely address other issues, bringing depth to the relationship. Ed Wheat calls committed love, "the Divine solution for marriages populated by imperfect human beings!"[10] All of us know so well our own imperfections! We need constant reassurance—security—that our spouses love us in spite of those imperfections.

Sometimes marriages face extremely difficult problems that test this security. Dave and Arlene Wilson are a good example. This couple belongs to the church I pastor in Washington state. For several years, I've had the privilege of observing their marriage relationship. I've keenly observed them especially because of the special circumstances that exist for this couple. You see, Arlene has multiple sclerosis, a chronic degenerative disease. As a result, many pressures have tested their commitment level.

Dave and Arlene's committed love has brought security to a relationship confronted by disease, and clearly, this couple faces difficult challenges. Since Arlene can no longer drive a car, Dave must transport her wherever she needs to go. As well, the multiple sclerosis makes Arlene sensitive to air temperature. I've witnessed Dave setting up fans at church so Arlene can be cool enough. This couple has endured a number of hospital stays and operations, each putting stress on both Arlene and Dave. What pressure this couple has had to bear!

When couples cannot perform well for each other, when expectations cannot be met, insecurity can begin to seep into a marriage relationship. However, instead of experiencing insecurity, I have watched Dave and Arlene make their relationship thrive. Their commitment to each other continues to bring them through this problem because their committed love has been unconditional, not tied to each other's performance. Dave and Arlene would be the first to tell you about their imperfections—they are only human—but committed love operating in their marriage has given them deep security and absence of fear.

Trust

If the bus comes at 4 P.M. on Monday, and again on Tuesday, Wednesday, and Thursday, you *trust* that it will come again on Friday at 4 P.M. You know you can count on it. In the same way, husbands and wives need to know that they can count on each other. Trust is foundational to the success of the relationship.

Why is trust so important? When you trust your spouse, you can open up and reveal yourself completely. Defenses come down. You don't have to put energy into protecting yourself because you trust that your spouse will not hurt or betray you. You can put aside the fear of failure, knowing that your spouse supports you 100 percent. You give your partner entrance to your heart, welcoming him or her to observe and share the complexity of your life together.

Listen to the telling words of a wife about trust:

> When we were first married, I became aware that I was keeping just a small part of myself from Lee, lest I become too vulnerable. One day, about three or four years into our marriage, I discovered that I fully trusted him, and that withholding was gone.[11]

When you know that you can trust your spouse, you can stop withholding your true self and become vulnerable. You know that you can count on your spouse's support and commitment no matter what your vulnerability reveals. Since

Naomi has demonstrated a rock-solid love for me, I trust her commitment without question. I *know* that if I mess up royally, she will never abandon me.

On more than one occasion in our first few years of marriage, I was insensitive to Naomi's needs. With my twenty-something confidence, I plowed ahead to do my own thing, ignoring her needs. She didn't reject me then, and she won't reject me at some point in the future. Since then, in countless ways, she has accepted me in spite of my weaknesses. I *know* that whatever I do, she will stay committed to me. I can't tell you what this trust has meant to our relationship. It has allowed us to open up to each other, to know and to be known.

Vision

As I talk to couples with healthy marriages, I often notice their sense of vision for the future. They envision a positive future for themselves as couples. They dream together about what they will do and how they will grow. They make plans together; they have goals. Norm Wright describes it this way: "Having a vision for your marriage is having a realistic dream for what you, your spouse, and your marriage can become under God's direction."[12]

Committed love gives your marriage relationship a future! You can dream together, looking ahead with positive feelings of warmth and anticipation. Instead of living day to day, hoping things work out, you can bank on your commitment and therefore picture yourselves working side by side, loving each other in the days to come.

When Naomi and I go away together, we enjoy looking ahead. Where is God taking us? What can we look forward to? We dream about where we will go for our twenty-fifth wedding anniversary or new ways to stay close. We work out goals for the future, saying essentially, "This is the way we want our marriage to be." Because of the committed love we demonstrate to each other, we have a positive view of the future together, a vision for our marriage.

Growth

Throughout my pastoral ministry I have worked with hundreds of couples in marriage counseling. Sadly, some of these couples did not grow in their relationships with each other. There were a number of reasons they didn't grow, but one stands out: They were not committed to each other. They learned new skills, but skills meant nothing without committed love. Commitment is like the gasoline that runs a car engine. You can have the most expensive car in the world, with the greatest engine and best tires, but unless you pour gasoline into it, that car will go nowhere! In the same way, without commitment—the fuel that powers the marital engine—skills won't take you anywhere.

On your wedding day, you possessed the raw materials for a wonderful relationship. To shape those raw materials into a work of art requires that you learn and practice skills that make for a great marriage. Committed love allows couples to stay focused on those skills, such as communication, positive conflict-resolution, and cooperation, among others. Commitment provides a safe environment for you to be in process as a couple. In fact, such a relationship is the ideal environment for interpersonal growth, too. David and Vera Mace said it this way: "In a [marriage] relationship in which we are fully known and also deeply loved, we can grow in a balanced fashion."[13]

My counseling experience with couples bears this out. I have spent many hundreds of hours as a pastoral counselor trying to help couples solve problems and grow in their marriage relationships. Because I strongly believe that God made us with the ability to change, I am usually optimistic about the counseling process. But without committed love, there is no marital growth or health. Without the will to do what it takes for a healthy relationship, no amount of instruction or skills will help.

Two couples I have seen recently in counseling illustrate this point. The first couple was in deep trouble, obviously at the end of the rope. As I spoke with the husband alone, I heard him say, "I don't know that I am committed any longer to this marriage. Until I make that decision, I suppose there's nothing to do." He was right, and sadly, the commitment never came.

A second couple asked me to help them grow as a couple. The husband and wife had endured many difficulties in their ten years of marriage. They realized that they needed more skill in building a strong relationship. As I worked with this husband and wife, their strong commitment to each other became apparent. They went to work and within three months had experienced significant growth in their relationship. Their commitment allowed the development of relational skills that benefited their marriage.

Committed love is the cornerstone that allows marital growth to take place. With it, couples can build a strong, vibrant relationship together. As you spend time together enriching your marriage, celebrate your commitment. It's a precious gift you give to each other.

Exercise: Looking Back to Your Vows[14]

As I have talked about the importance of committed love in this chapter, you may wonder, "What's the most important way in which I can demonstrate such commitment?" There is no one answer to that question. As you look at a rich and intricate painting, how can you say which brush stroke was the most important in creating the beauty you observe? Every act of kindness, every choice to affirm, every active sharing of yourself with each other collaborate to create a beautiful marriage based on committed love.

Let me suggest one way you can, during this weekend, enrich your relationship around this vital idea of committed love. This activity centers on your initial act of commitment to each other. Listen to Mike Mason's words:

> Marriages which consistently look back to their vows, to those wild promises made before God, and which trust Him to make sense out of them, find a continual source of strength and renewal.[15]

I agree! You can enrich and renew your marriage by returning to the promises that began your relationship. For a few moments on your weekend together, look back to your vows. Read to each other those "wild promises," and deliberately affirm them once again. If you don't have your own vows handy, read the vows below, inserting your names into the appropriate blanks as you read.

> "I,__________, take thee,__________, to be my wedded __________, to have and to hold from this day forward; for better or worse, for richer or poorer, in sickness and in health, to love, to honor, and to cherish, so long as we both shall live, according to God's holy ordinance, and thereto I give you my pledge."

Notice that these vows have five elements (if you have them handy, look at your own vows for the elements included in them):

1. a choice to freely enter into marriage;
2. a promise to pursue the relationship through all physical, financial, or psychological challenges;
3. a commitment to love for a lifetime;

4. a commitment to honor for a lifetime; and
5. a commitment to cherish for a lifetime.

This means that whatever crisis arises your commitment to each other will not waver. Marriage vows say that even when you don't see eye to eye with each other, you will treat each other with respect and honor. You promise to be loyal and faithful. You vow to cherish each other, promising personal affection and deep friendship. You commit to paying attention to those things that will build up each other. And the implications for these vows go on and on.

Here's want I would like for you to do in this exercise:

1. Individually, update your vows, making them speak for today. Take a pen and paper and put the concepts into a few short and memorable sentences. Be creative! Have fun! Don't feel intimidated—your spouse doesn't expect a masterpiece, just a heartfelt expression of your love.

   Here's an example: "I chose to marry you, and I'm glad I did! I'd marry you all over again. Whatever happens, you have my heart. I'm committed to love you all of my life. I'm going to honor you in the way I speak and in the way I act. I'm going to cherish you in my heart and become your best friend. I'm committed to this marriage, but I'm also committed to you. I'm yours, now and forever."
2. When you've finished writing, come together and say your renewed vows to each other.
3. Spend a moment in prayer, thanking God for each other and asking Him to help you experience a renewal of committed love.

4. When you come home from your weekend away, say these updated vows to each other two or three times a week for the next three months.

Now turn to Appendix B, "Our Commitment to Marriage Enrichment" (page 184) and, in the space provided, jot down insights you've gained from this chapter and changes you could make to further enrich your marriage.

CHAPTER FIVE

Foundation 2: Skillful Communication

Doug and Amber had a good marriage relationship. They were deeply committed, wonderfully caring, and firmly resolved to grow closer together. They had one problem, however, that kept intruding into their relationship. Amber often did not feel listened to. Doug was a man of action, someone who made decisions quickly and had strong opinions. Amber was more reflective, less able to assertively express her desires. As a result, she would often indicate a desire that Doug might totally overlook. She felt, more often than not, that he ignored her desires. This wasn't because Doug didn't care but because he didn't have the skills necessary to really listen to his wife. For this couple to grow together, they needed to learn some simple communication skills: He needed to learn to listen, and she needed to learn to clearly request what she really wanted.

This couple attended a marriage-enrichment weekend I led some years ago. Fortunately, they discovered what impeded their growth as a couple and learned the rudimentary skills they needed to break through the barrier that had hindered them for so long. Three years later, this couple continues to experience the positive effects of these simple but effective communication skills. Doug and Amber enriched their marriage by taking the time to examine and develop their communication skills.

Most couples could find a substantial benefit from a communication tuneup. We often take for granted the skills necessary for a good relationship, as if they were automatic. Not true! Good communication takes effort and practice. Before this chapter is finished, I'll offer three simple skills that will make a difference in your relationship, and you can practice them as you spend time together this weekend.

As you read Chapters 5 and 6, don't be intimidated by the length! Remember that each chapter takes a maximum of forty-five minutes to read aloud or thirty minutes to read silently. You'll find the format easy to follow and the material helpful for your marriage.

Communication and Intimacy

Spouses sometimes feel stymied about this whole business of marital intimacy. They want to feel close and be best friends, yet they don't know how to make that happen. If you want to enrich your marriage and encourage intimacy in your relationship, you need to know one fact: Communication and intimacy are linked.

In marriages where the intimacy level grows, a simple interaction happens over and over: Husbands and wives choose to risk by disclosing who they are, and in return, their partners offer understanding and acceptance. This interaction goes back and forth, year in and year out. It does more, by itself, to deepen intimacy in a marriage than almost anything else. Couples who want their intimacy level to increase must risk self-disclosure.

When I talk about self-disclosure, I can almost feel husbands closing down. Does sharing oneself mean you must share every thought that comes into your head, exposing yourself in inappropriate ways? No way! John Stewart, a professor of communication, offers a good definition of self-disclosure:

> Genuine self-disclosure simply means honestly sharing something of who you actually are with someone else, something that others would be unlikely to know unless you tell them.[1]

Husband, did you hear? Self-disclosure is just sharing yourself with your wife. It's talking about your life, your thoughts, your emotions—things your wife would not know unless you told her.

Of course, disclosing who you are isn't enough. As you self-disclose, your wife must give understanding and acceptance. What's more, she must *communicate* that understanding and acceptance. The Bible says, "The purposes of a man's heart are deep waters, but a man of understanding draws them out" (Proverbs 20:5). When a wife communicates understanding by listening, creating a safe environment, she reaps the reward of her husband's deepest thoughts.

Naomi has done this for me many times. Not long ago, Naomi inadvertently hurt me by something she said. I thought I could overlook it, but over the next few minutes, I found my feelings persisting. Finally, Naomi noticed the tension and asked me what was going on. As I told her about my feelings, she listened carefully. She drew out my deepest thoughts because she wisely listened without judgment. I felt—and was—safe to say what was on my mind.

This really works both ways. If you make an effort to listen carefully to each other, understanding each other's thoughts and accepting each other's ideas (even if you don't agree), you'll encourage each other to go to the next level of self-disclosure. You'll be surprised at what you'll say to each other when you both know that the other will try to understand and accept what you say.

Levels of Communication

John Powell's work on levels of communication can help us understand how we relate to each other.[2] Powell maintains that when we communicate, we do so on one of five levels. These levels begin with those requiring little or no self-disclosure and progress to those requiring deep honesty and self-revelation. Intimate marriage relationships happen when both partners feel safe to reveal who they really are, to communicate on the deepest level of self-disclosure.

Powell's five levels are listed below:

> Level One: The Cliche. We communicate on this level when we say phrases such as "How are you?"; "I like your hair"; and "Nice weather we're having." This kind of communication requires no sharing of the inner person. There's no risk and no intimacy gained.

> Level Two: Reporting Facts. The conversation on this level sounds like this: "Did you hear what happened today?" and "Today at work I...." You share the facts and nothing but the facts. While you share on a bit of a deeper level, this level still requires little risk.

> Level Three: Sharing Ideas and Opinions. This level is where the risk really begins. Any time you say, "This is what I think," you risk evaluation and rejection. Intimate communication begins as you share your true thoughts.

> Level Four: Communicating Emotions. This level goes

even deeper. A wife might say, "I'm feeling so great about our new house," or a husband might say, "I'm scared about losing my job." Sharing emotions deepens intimacy as you reveal how you react emotionally to situations and circumstances.

Level Five: Complete Emotional Openness. On this level, spouses, with total honesty, reveal their thoughts, emotions, and attitudes. This includes what they think or feel about each other; for example, "When you come home late without calling, I feel angry" or "I feel so proud of you when you put God first." These open and honest statements enhance intimacy as they're predicated on an expectation of acceptance.

Where Couples Live

Couples don't always find it easy to communicate at those deepest levels. Jason told me recently:

> At forty-four years of age, I still have this fear of rejection, fear of telling my wife something that I'm ashamed of, or emotions that I feel are dumb or inappropriate for me to have. It's an area in our marriage that needs attention.

Jason has a good marriage, but he still needs work in this area.

Right now, ask yourselves, "On what level do we most often communicate?" If you communicate primarily on the cliche and reporting-facts levels, your relationship has a lot of room for growth. If you often communicate on the three deepest levels, you have a great foundation to experience an even deeper relationship.

Three Communication Skills That Work

When I help couples deepen their marriage relationships, I have the joy of hearing weekly progress reports. I often hear comments such as "It's been such a good week. We don't know exactly what happened, but it was great." My comments to these couples are always the same: "Hold it. When you have a positive week there are reasons. You must ask yourself the question, 'What is it that we did to give ourselves a great week?' Nothing happens by accident! You had a great week because you made some choices to use the skills you possess."

I have identified three skills that have helped other couples and can help you deepen your relationship: active listening, sharing, and asking. Yes, they require a bit of work, but as you work on these skills you'll enrich your marriage and deepen your communication level.

Skill 1: Active Listening

Listening to our spouses is hard for one simple reason: We all have a natural tendency to evaluate and judge what our partners say, filtering their words through our own points of view. If, for example, one of you says, "I really think it's time we invested in the stock market with our savings," the other will most likely form some kind of evaluative response such as "That's a great idea" or "That's a risky idea." The hearer might even make a judgment such as "My spouse is a really good thinker" or "I don't think my spouse has a good grasp on our finances." Many communication experts believe that this automatic evaluation response creates a major barrier to communication.

What's wrong with using our minds, you ask? Nothing at all. There is a time for expressing our rational thoughts. But when we rush too quickly to evaluate, not only do we miss what our spouse is saying, we fail to communicate that we really are listening. You know what I mean. How many times has your spouse been talking and you can't wait to respond? Instead of listening carefully, you rehearse what you'll say when you get the chance!

John Gray makes the point that men often find listening more difficult because they have a different psychological makeup than women. Men need to understand what follows:

> When a woman needs to talk about feelings, she generally needs a man to listen with empathy. At those times, she wants him to understand that she is not looking for his help in solving her problems but just wants to feel his emotional support. When he gives his solutions, she instinctively says, "You don't understand."[3]

I have had to learn and relearn this with my wife, Naomi, over the years. Naomi and I are in pastoral ministry together, and sometimes Naomi feels overwhelmed with her duties. Once in a while, she wants to blow off steam. When she does, my usual response is to develop a solution: "Honey, just say no to that responsibility" or "You've got to tell that person you can't do it." But when I do that, Naomi usually shuts down and says something like "It's OK, Art. I'm just complaining." She doesn't want my solutions—she wants my ear! I'm a slow learner, but I'm finally beginning to get it!

We have a good example for listening in our heavenly Father. Listen to the Psalmist: "I love the LORD, because he hears me; he listens to my prayers" (Psalm 116:1 GNB). God is a listener, and He sets an example for us in listening to our spouses. The book of Proverbs also teaches us about listening. Proverbs 18 cuts most quickly to this issue: "He who answers before listening—that is his folly and his shame" (Proverbs 18:13). Ouch! God's Word says "listen." This is a crucial skill in enriching your marriage and one in which you can continue to grow.

As you listen to your spouse, especially initially, you need to put aside solutions and evaluation for the time being and concentrate on really hearing your partner. How is this done? With a skill known as active listening. Let me give you some information about communication that will help you develop this skill.

Most messages have two components. Both husbands and wives need to understand that active listening begins with understanding the total nature of a message. Many messages we receive from our spouses have both a *content* and an *emotional* component. For example, suppose you are ready to leave for church and one of you asks, "Are you ready to go yet?" What is the content? A simple question—are you ready to go? However, based on the phrasing and tone of the question, you could hear a variety of emotional elements to the message. If you emphasize the word "yet," you may communicate anger. Say the whole sentence with a slightly raised voice, and you may communicate extreme frustration. On the other hand, if you say the sentence in a normal tone, the emotional component of the message may be neutral.

Misreading the emotional component of your spouse's communication can be disastrous. Hearing the whole message, however—both content and emotion—helps your partner feel heard, and that's what active listening is all about.

Active listening consists of three parts:

1. attending,
2. reflecting, and
3. confirming.

Attending is the simple art of paying attention. This means first that you physically attend to your spouse. You orient your body to him or her. You sit or stand not more than two and a half feet away. You make sure that nonverbally—through gestures, posture, and facial expressions—you indicate that you are listening.

Attending also means maintaining eye contact. This is so important! When couples are having trouble they tend to withhold eye contact, and believe me, such withholding clearly communicates distance. But when you maintain eye contact, you demonstrate that you are paying attention. Even our children know this. When my children were preschoolers, they would sometimes pull my head toward them when they wanted to tell me something. They wanted to see my eyes so they knew they had my attention!

When you listen to your spouse, give fairly constant eye contact. The speaker will sometimes look away, and that's OK. In our society, constant eye contact is uncomfortable. However, the listener should maintain focus.

Finally, attend with your inner attitude. When your spouse needs to talk, give your spouse your full attention. Communicate that you'll be there for as long as it takes to really enter your spouse's world. Your spouse will know if you're willing to suspend judgment and really try to understand him or her. This attitude comes through loud and clear.

Reflecting is the second step of active listening. It consists of paraphrasing—putting into your own words—what you hear your spouse saying. You reflect two things: first, the content, and second, the emotion behind the communication. I call this skill reflecting because it's like a relational mirror. When you look into a mirror, you see what's there. The mirror doesn't add new information; it merely reflects back what it sees. In the same way, paraphrasing centers on reflecting back what has actually been said, not adding new information. Reflecting is the art of recognizing the core—content and emotion—of your spouse's message.

Couples who reflect what they hear use these kinds of phrases:

1. What I hear you saying is....
2. Are you saying...?
3. Let me understand. What you were feeling was....
4. What I'm hearing is that....
5. Sounds like you feel....

Statements that begin with these kinds of leads indicate an attempt to really listen. You put in your own words the main idea and emotion you hear. You don't parrot, repeating verbatim everything you hear. Instead, you boil down what you hear to the most important parts, using usually no more than one or two sentences.

Listen for a moment to this wife speak to her husband: "I have been feeling far away from you recently. We haven't had much time together. I'm not complaining—I know you've been busy. I guess I wonder how it can change. I really want to be close to you. The schedule has really gotten in the way."

The husband responds, "Sounds like, because of our schedules, you've been feeling distanced from me, maybe lonely? You want to figure out a way to change it?"

"That's right. Can we talk about it?"

This husband didn't mechanically repeat back what he heard. Instead, he reflected the main idea and emotion in two brief sentences. He demonstrated that he really did understand what his wife said. Imagine for a moment that instead of reflecting what he had heard, this husband had said something like "Well, we can't really do anything about it now" or "Don't be so upset—we'll get over this." Those responses would have shut down his wife.

Consider this husband speaking to his wife: "Honey, I'm

concerned about something going on in our relationship. It seems that nothing I do is ever good enough for you. I try and try, but you never seem pleased with me. Sometimes I feel like giving up, but I know that's wrong. I just don't know what to do."

"I think I'm hearing you say that it's very hard to please me, and you don't know what to do about it. Is that it?"

"That's right. We've got to figure out a way to move past this."

Obviously, such a conversation would have a long way to go to come to solutions; however, this wife demonstrated an initial willingness to listen to her husband.

In fact, that's the main reason for paraphrasing your spouse's words: Paraphrasing *demonstrates* that you were really listening. It lets your spouse know that you've paid attention! If you can get to the heart of your spouse's words and reflect that back, you project incredible affirmation. You demonstrate that you really understand, that you care enough to listen.

Confirming is the last step in active listening. It completes the communication loop. The person who originally spoke lets the listener know that he or she has indeed understood. The speaker does this by nodding or saying, "Yes" or "That's right." However, if the listener has *not* heard accurately, the speaker has a chance to say something like, "That's partly right, but what was most important to me was...." At this point, the listener tries again and keeps trying until he or she has heard the main idea and any emotion present.

Active listening is a great skill, one that takes work to do well. Should you use it during every interaction between you? Not at all. A plumber may have many tools in his toolbox, from hammers to hacksaws. He uses some tools more often than others, but no one tool is used for everything. In the same way, active listening is a basic "tool" that you'll use often but not on all occasions. You'll want to use active listening when you have any tension, conflict, or confusion between you. You'll also want to actively listen any time you realize that your spouse is saying something particularly important to him or her, especially if he or she is sharing feelings.

To use a tool properly, you need to practice with it. You'll have an opportunity to practice the active-listening skill during the exercises that follow this chapter. But before proceeding to the next section, tell each other one time that you felt the other did an excellent job of listening.

Skill 2: Sharing

In a recent secular poll, husbands and wives agreed that "the ability to talk to each other about feelings" was one of the most important components of a good marriage.[4] This study affirmed the vital importance of communicating on an emotional level. To enrich and deepen your marriage, both of you must learn to share yourselves with each other.

Many times, husbands tell me, "I just don't know how to share this part of my life." Sometimes women are reluctant, too, because of past rejection or other hurts. Despite your natural inclination or your past experiences, you can learn this skill! As you provide each other a safe environment, giving understanding and acceptance, you both can move ahead in sharing thoughts, ideas, and emotions.

The first step in sharing is learning to recognize what's going on inside you. One of the problems with sharing is that often husbands (and sometimes wives) don't know what they're feeling. Instead of examining his emotions, a husband will tend to intellectualize or simply ignore what's going on inside him. Of course, these feelings do come out later through withdrawal and various other indirect methods of communication.

Then, too, sometimes couples are afraid of emotions. One husband confessed this to me:

> In a class we took, the instructor said that there is no such things as bad emotions but only bad ways of handling emotions. I have struggled with that concept because of the Christian ideas that you need to be strong and not have worry or doubt or anger.

When you are afraid of emotions, especially negative ones, you tend not to listen to your real feelings. Thus you have a more difficult time knowing where you are emotionally.

To overcome this dilemma, Christian counselor David Carlson has helped couples recognize their feelings with six words that incorporate most emotions.[5] He uses the acronym "SASHET" to help couples remember some basic feeling words. The acronym stands for the following words:

1. Scared
2. Angry
3. Sad
4. Happy
5. Excited
6. Tender

Carlson certainly recognizes that many feeling words may come under each of these basic six. For example, "warm-hearted," "loving," and "gentle" might all come under the word "tender." The point is that these words give couples a way to process their feelings by first helping them identify their *basic* emotions. Recognizing the emotions is a beginning step.

How then does a husband or wife share such feelings? When you have become aware of your feelings, there are two steps in communicating them. *First, share the context for your feelings—the events or situations which led to your feelings.* For example, "I'm very tired tonight" or "Today one of the people I work with complimented me." *Second, after explaining the context, simply share the emotions you've been feeling.* If you wish, you can communicate these using the SASHET acronym. You can also use word pictures to deepen the impression. For example, "I feel as if my best friend has just turned against me" would clearly communicate a deep sadness.

This two-step process for sharing feelings can be reduced to this phrase: "I feel…because…." For example, "I feel disappointed because I messed up at work today." If you can remember this simple phrase, it will help you describe both the context for your emotions and the feelings themselves.

Most close couples use the two-step process to share with each other on a regular basis. Recently, I said to Naomi, "What with this hay fever going full bore, and all the commitments I'm obligated to in the next several weeks, I'm feeling overwhelmed." I shared a very simple bit of information, but it was so vital to our relationship. Whenever you share these kinds of statements with each other, you let each other into your world. As a result, you draw closer to each other.

Sharing with our spouses is biblical. It serves as an extension of the "one flesh" covenant we have made with our spouses. God intends marriage to be an intimate bond. When Adam said to Eve, "This is now bone of my bones and flesh of my flesh" (Genesis 2:23), those were *feeling* words, not just facts. Adam expressed an inner emotion and set a precedence of intimacy for all marriages.

Men must give more attention to sharing on a deep level. Women more naturally share their deepest selves with their husbands than their husbands do with them. Men have to work at it. Norm Wright suggests why this is so:

> Men tend to be like medieval castles of olden days. We erect walls and moats for protection. Why? One reason

> for limiting emotional expression is our way of staying in control. Men have a driving need to be in charge and they like to decide who can enter into their lives and when. These walls hide hurts, joys, frustrations, fear, guilt, sorrows and...even love.[6]

Husbands, you must learn to bring down those walls. This means that you consciously decide to share your thoughts and feelings. It may mean that like many couples, you choose a time in the day when you can talk with your wives, and you keep that appointment—every day. However you do it, work to bring down those walls.

Women can help their husbands listen to them when they want to share. Yes, it's true! A couple that I worked with recently had a problem. Earl and Maggie were ready to deepen their relationship when they came to me, and they made considerable progress in their relationship over three months. One small problem that they recognized during our time together was that Earl often felt blamed or frustrated when Maggie shared negative feelings, even though these feelings weren't usually directed at him. Maggie might have shared frustration about an interaction with one of the children's teachers or anxiety about her part-time job. But Earl often assumed that her negative feelings were somehow aimed at him, and he became defensive. At that point, he couldn't actively listen to Maggie, and many times an argument would begin.

But during our time together, Earl learned that all Maggie really wanted was simply for him to listen to and understand her. So he learned to listen carefully and empathetically with frequent feedback. At times, Earl would ask Maggie if she wanted help with the problem. This gave her the opportunity to garner his suggestions if she wanted them. And Maggie learned to prepare Earl for what she had to say. She might say, "I want to tell you about my day. I know that you can't do anything about my frustration, but it sure would make me feel better if I could share what's going on with me." With preparation, Earl began to relax and really listen to what his wife shared.

Husbands, pay attention to this: If your wife cannot share her negative feelings with you, she will feel abandoned. In most cases, her negative emotions aren't aimed at you. So unless she talks directly about your behavior, don't assume that she's talking about you! Instead, listen actively as she shares.

The "check-in" is a useful mechanism by which countless couples have learned to stay current with each other emotionally. Some marriage partners find it more difficult to share their inner world with their spouses. If this is the case for you or your spouse, the check-in makes it easier to access and share that deep part of your lives. This simple suggestion is easy to use and creates an open door for you and your spouse to be vulnerable about thoughts and feelings.

The skill consists of asking one simple question: "How are you doing?" When a spouse asks this question, it becomes an offer for his or her partner to open up a bit and share what's going on inside. The question, of course, might vary. Here are some variations on the theme: "What are you thinking?"; "What are you feeling?"; "Are you OK?"; "Tell me about your day. What happened?" These questions tell your spouse that you're available to listen to whatever he or she has to say. Naomi and I often use this skill two or three times during the day, sometimes over the phone, sometimes in person. It helps us stay connected and current with each other; you can reap the same benefit if you put it into practice often, too.

Couples must make time to talk and share on many levels. James Dobson has stated the bottom line here: "Time must be reserved for meaningful conversation."[7] Certainly this includes sharing emotions, but we should also broaden "meaningful conversation" to include all five levels of communication. Facts, ideas and opinions, and emotions all have a place. Couples must make time to talk about their lives, their dreams, their struggles. Couples can begin to feel distant very quickly unless they have a regular means of keeping track of each other.

One husband I talked to found this out early in his marriage: "Sometimes I would do some chore for my wife to show her how much I loved her. That's not what she wanted. She wanted me to sit down and talk to her." Conversation needs to happen every day. Remember that self-disclosure simply means honestly sharing something of who you actually are with your spouse. How will your spouse know who you are unless you tell him or her?

Believe me, when you learn to share with each other, communicating on a deep level, you'll do one of the best things you can possibly do to strengthen and develop your marriage. You'll bind your hearts together, virtually guaranteeing the rich blessings of an intimate marriage.

Pause for a minute to nail down the last time you shared on this intimate level with each other. Affirm each other for expressing yourselves so deeply.

Skill 3: Asking

One of the positive aspects of a successful marriage is that each partner feels free to ask for what he or she wants or needs. Some couples find this difficult to do. I've often observed, however, that when couples don't have this skill, spouses tend to ask for what they want *indirectly.* Worse, someone holds a need inside for a long time, then his or her anger ferments and erupts later. Neither option is a healthy way to express a need.

Think about it. Can your spouse read your mind? Sometimes wives say to me, "If he loved me, he'd figure it out." Not necessarily true! If you want to enrich your relationship, you must be able to ask for what you want or need.

Men, however, can be even worse, especially in areas that assail their pride. The area of sexuality is a good example. Many men find it difficult to ask for sex. They do it indirectly by making romantic advances. However, if their wives don't enthusiastically return their advances, the husbands back off. They feel rebuffed and may withdraw. Instead of making a request for sex directly, they spend the next few hours working through their "rejection."

Husbands and wives need to learn to speak directly and make requests. Here's a simple formula you can use: "I need/would like...because...." In practice this technique might sound something like this: "It would help me if you could take Jon to his ball practices the next two Saturdays because my schedule is absolutely packed." Or this: "I'd appreciate it if you could phone me once during your workday because it gives me a chance to check in with you." Or a husband might say this: "Judy, it would really mean a lot to me if we could make love tonight. I've been thinking about you all day."

Of course, when one of you asks for something, the other really needs to listen and carefully consider the request. If one of you has taken a risk and admitted a need, the other should do his or her best to consider how to help. When this happens, you strengthen your relationship.

Do either of you have a need or desire to communicate to each other? If so, take the time—and the risk—to do so right now.

Change Takes Time

These three skills work! But remember, real change takes time. New skills may seem artificial and difficult at first, but after time and practice, they can become regular patterns. Do you remember learning to drive? If you've been through this process, then you probably remember your first timid attempts. When you first got into the car, you looked cautiously around, then turned the key and started the motor. After a few seconds, you hesitantly put the car into reverse, then slowly backed out of the driveway. Everything felt strange; you over steered and over braked! Now, years later, look at yourself! You hop in the car, have it started and backed out literally *without thinking about it!* These skills have been burned into your motor patterns. All it took was time, motivation, and practice. In the same way, you can develop the communication skills I've described.

Now that you've read this chapter, pick one or both of the exercises below and have fun working through them. Think of these exercises as a way of deepening your relationship and enriching your marriage.

Exercise 1: Active-Listening Skills

Here's a quick review. The elements of active listening are:

1. *Attending:* As the speaker shares, the listener orients his or her body position toward the speaker, maintains eye contact, and focuses attention on the speaker.

2. *Reflecting:* When the speaker has finished sharing, the listener paraphrases the content of and the emotion (if any) contained in the message. Remember, "What I hear you saying is...."

3. *Confirming:* After the paraphrase, the speaker affirms that the listener's restatement is accurate, or if not, clarifies the original message—without adding to it.

Now that you've refreshed your memory, use the questions below to practice the active-listening skill. One of you speaks first, the other attends and paraphrases, then the speaker confirms. After you've successfully practiced active listening once, reverse roles.

If this is a new skill for you, try to paraphrase your spouse's statements after every four or five sentences. If you have some familiarity with this skill, use this opportunity to practice what you know and help your spouse feel listened to! If this exercise develops into a discussion, great!

This skill may be difficult at first. That's OK. Just do the best you can to reflect the main idea and any emotion that you hear.

Discussion Questions:

1. Are you able to self-disclose as you want to? Is sharing on deeper levels hard or easy for you? Why or why not?
2. How would you describe yourself as a listener?
3. How could the content of this chapter make a difference in our marriage relationship? What changes could we make in light of this material?
4. Is there something you'd like to say about this element of communication but haven't had a chance to say in the past? If so, what?

Exercise 2: Sharing Feelings

Complete the sentences below, elaborating as much as you need. Takes turns sharing. Remember to actively listen to each other.

1. If I could go back and relive a special memory with you it would be....
2. The times when I feel closest to you are....
3. When I think about the future with you, I most look forward to....
4. When I reflect on your love for me and commitment to me, I feel....

Now turn to Appendix B, "Our Commitment to Marriage Enrichment" (page 184) and, in the space provided, jot down insights you've gained from this chapter and changes you could make to further enrich your marriage.

CHAPTER SIX

Foundation 3: Effective Conflict Resolution

Understanding Conflict

Should you talk about conflict on a romantic weekend away? Absolutely! I recently spent an evening with five happily married couples. Each husband-and-wife pair talked about the deeply satisfying nature of their relationship. Do you know what every one of these couples said to me? "Conflict is a part of our relationship!"

Are you surprised? You shouldn't be. Conflict is an inevitable part of every marriage. In fact, couples can't have healthy and growing relationships without good means for handling conflict. If couples don't process their conflicts, they can't work through their differences to new levels of intimacy.

Married couples experience conflict because of the tension inherent in *two* unique people forming *one* marital partnership. Think about it. Each of you has a different background and temperament. Each of you has a different perspective, different interests, and different preferences. To top it all off, one of you is male, and one of you is female! With all these differences, no wonder husbands and wives disagree at times!

Conflict, Not Fighting

I'm not saying, however, that *fighting* is inevitable. Make no mistake: Conflict is *not* the same as fighting! Conflict is simply what happens when two people disagree. The disagreement may be about how to discipline the kids, what color you'd like to paint the living room, where you'll go for vacation, or whether to send out Christmas cards this year! In successful marriages, husbands and wives resolve such disagreements. In unsuccessful marriages, they don't.

Conflict happens within all marriages. The variable then is *how* a husband and wife handle their conflicts. Will they avoid conflict? Will one partner try to win, regardless of the cost to his or her spouse? If a husband and wife deal with conflict in these or other destructive ways, they'll destroy their marriage relationship. On the other hand, if a couple goes through a process of mutual adaptation—resolving conflict while placing a high value upon the relationship—a marriage can actually *grow* through conflict!

Stop and reflect briefly. How does the way you handle conflict affect your relationship with each other? Are you helping or hindering the growth process?

Marriage experts David and Vera Mace make this observation: "Marriage is a continuing struggle to turn…the inevitable conflicts that arise in every close relationship into growth points for the improvement of the relationship."[1] Turning conflicts into growth points—that's the challenge. When it happens, couples are far more likely to experience health and wholeness in their marriages.

God Has Something to Say

Enriching our marriages as God designs requires a biblical method of conflict resolution. And communicating your concerns to each other *is* biblical. Jesus said it this way: "Show him his fault, just between the two of you" (Matthew 18:15). Jesus made it clear: Take care of the issue! Don't ignore it—do something about it!

The *way* you talk about an issue makes a big difference! Listen to this encouragement from God's Word: "The wise in heart are called discerning, and pleasant words promote instruction" (Proverbs 16:21). God says that if we are spiritually wise, we will learn to communicate in ways that will promote instruction. If you're wise, you'll learn to communicate even negative emotions in ways that make it possible for you to hear each other. "Pleasant words" will help you listen to and understand each other.

Handle the process with concern for each other's welfare, with the attitude of "building [them] up according to their needs" (Ephesians 4:29), and you'll move in the right direction!

The Negative Conflict Cycle

As you read this chapter, I want to help you develop a few practical skills for successfully resolving conflict. Before that, however, you must recognize a common syndrome in handling conflict that hinders many married couples. This negative process can intrude time and again in the midst of conflict. It derails the resolution of the problem at hand and leaves the scars of marital warfare upon both partners. I want to describe this cycle to you because if you can recognize it, you can deal with it. And you can avoid it by developing positive conflict-resolution skills.

The negative conflict cycle begins with blame. Perhaps a wife tells her husband: "You never listen to me! You're always playing golf or working on the computer. Why are you so insensitive?" Blame absolutely erupts from these words. Notice that the word "you" is used three times. Such "you statements" tend to point a finger of blame. Also look at the label the wife uses: "insensitive." To top it off, she uses the hot-button words "never," "always," and "why." Unless this woman's husband is superhuman, he'll feel blamed when confronted in this manner.

When a person feels blamed, he or she will most likely kick into the second step in the negative conflict cycle: defensiveness. Defensive behavior is simply behavior that occurs when you perceive a threat. You want to protect yourself, to defend against the stinging indictments of hurtful words. Interestingly, research has shown that "defense arousal prevents the listener from concentrating upon the message."[2] In other words, when a husband or wife feels blamed, he or she has a much harder time of listening to the original complaint.

Defensiveness usually works itself out in one of three ways. Think about it in your own life for a moment. What do *you* do when you feel blamed? First, you might decide to counter-blame, telling your spouse how he or she is ultimately responsible for the complaint. This combative reaction has the immediate affect of pushing those ugly words away by striking back. Second, you might react by simply defending yourself: "I am *not* insensitive. Why just last week I asked how I could help you with your workload." This reaction signals that you are entering into battle. Third, if you prefer to avoid conflict, you might withdraw. You just clam up and move away.

The problem with all of these defensive reactions is that they tend to give one message to your spouse: "I'm not listening!" If you counter-blame, your spouse may come on even stronger. If you defend, he or she will think you're not really getting the picture. If you withdraw, your spouse will feel abandoned. When you choose any of these options, the original speaker doesn't feel listened to and will tend to escalate. By this time, neither spouse feels heard, and the conflict certainly isn't resolved. And unless you resolve your conflict, the negative conflict cycle will go in circles—blame and defensiveness, blame and defensiveness—solving nothing and producing a world of pain.

This chapter is designed to help you avoid such ineffective means of handling conflict. To enrich your marriage, use this chapter to fine-tune your conflict-resolution skills. I think you'll find some helpful ideas no matter how you currently handle conflict.

Three Skills That Help Resolve Conflict

There are three conflict-resolution skills that any couple can use to enrich their marriage. When couples use these skills, they can turn their conflicts into growth opportunities for their marriages. As you practice these skills, your ability to handle conflict will take a big leap forward.

Each of these skills reflects the following principle found in God's Word: "Do not let any unwholesome talk come out of your mouths, but only what is helpful for building others up according to their needs, that it may benefit those who listen" (Ephesians 4:29). When you speak kindly and directly to each other about negative issues, you help build each other up, and you open the door to resolving your issues. I believe that the skills below are "wholesome" ways to talk to each other and will move you along in resolving conflict.

1. The "SAFE" Strategy[3]

A skill central to handling conflict is the ability to communicate negative emotions without blame or without withholding feelings. When used as the first step in conflict resolution, the SAFE strategy can make a tremendous difference in creating a positive tone for the process to come. SAFE is an acrostic, each letter standing for a word; I've described each element of the strategy below.

Sins—The first step in the SAFE strategy is to *cover* for one another's *sins*. The idea here is suggested from 1 Peter 4:8: "Love covers over a multitude of sins." ("Sin" in this strategy may be too strong a word in all cases. In many instances you might be concerned about a difference of opinion or a personality issue. However, the strategy is still the same.) Covering for each other means that, as you begin to speak about something that's bothering you, you let each other know of your love regardless of the problem. You don't express blame; instead, you express your desire to understand.

Let's say that one of you has been heavily involved at work recently, somewhat neglecting your part in caring for the children. The other of you decides to address the issue, beginning a conversation with the following words: "Honey, I know that the project you've been working on is important to you…" By beginning your confrontation this way, what have you done? You've said, "I understand that you're human. I know that your work has sidetracked you. I'm willing to cover for you."

The key phrases in this step are "I know…" and "I understand…" Why? Because they let your spouse know that you won't reject him or her, that you're trying to understand why he or she has let you down. This kind of discussion-starter also assures your spouse that you're trying to see things from his or her point of view. Essentially, these phrases help your spouse receive your words.

Actions—Next, *describe* your partner's *actions*; the behaviors that concern you. This is an important and difficult task, one that many couples tend to botch. Instead of describing actions, spouses often label them. A label says what your partner *is*; a description of actions says what your partner *does*. There's a world of difference between the two! When your husband, for example, is late for dinner, you might be tempted to label his behavior as "insensitive" or "inconsiderate." When your wife is doing a project and has her materials spread all over the kitchen for days, the word "messy" might come to mind! But you must resist the temptation to label. Labels are like waving a red flag in front of a bull. You actually invite your partner to charge! Do everything you can to resist labeling your spouse because a label is synonymous with blame, and it can send you into the negative conflict cycle.

Instead of labeling, describe your partner's actions. For example, it's 7 P.M., and your spouse hasn't arrived home from work yet. He or she hasn't called, and when he or she does arrive home, dinner has waited, growing cold, for twenty minutes. When you discuss the problem, you begin by covering for him or her: "I know how easy it is for you to lose track of time." Then, describe your spouse's actions: "But when you come home late and do not call...." You encourage conflict resolution when you describe actions because you don't wave the red flag of blame and invite a negative reaction. You do, however, clearly state the problem behavior and talk about the issue.

The key phrases in this step are "when you..." or "when I see you...." These words introduce a description of the behavior that concerns you.

Feelings—After describing your partner's actions, *disclose* what *feelings* those actions have elicited from you. This is an important part of resolving the conflict. Your partner must know what is going on inside you. Your spouse must hear your heart. As you share your feelings, you give your spouse a handle on the issue's importance to you. You help your spouse understand the impact of his or her actions. And by expressing your negative emotions directly, you are much less likely to make indirect statements or have your anger build.

Remember that revealing your feelings to your spouse is an intimate behavior. Disclosing negative emotions is, after all, a risk. By revealing your feelings, you say, "I trust you." By sharing your inner world, you draw closer to your spouse.

Let's say that your spouse has a tendency to joke about you at social gatherings. He or she doesn't mean any malice, but you feel bad about it. You want to tell your spouse how the joking affects you. Of course, you start by covering for your spouse: "Honey, I understand that when you're talking with our friends you tend to be spontaneous...." Then you continue with a description of the behavior that concerns you: "But when you joke about one of my faults with others...." Now comes the time to disclose your feelings: "I feel embarrassed and sad." If you want to, you may add a "because" to this phrase to give more context for the feeling: "I feel embarrassed and sad because I wonder how much you really value me."

Please don't turn the expression of feelings into a "you statement," a statement that centers on your spouse. It's easy to do this. For example, "I feel that *you* are being insensitive." That's not an emotion! It's a way of blaming your spouse by labeling him or her. Remember, communicate your feelings, not your spouse's faults as you see them. "I feel you..." is a phrase you should avoid using. The way to say something about your partner's behavior is to describe it, then disclose how that behavior made you feel.

You might want to consider using a word picture to communicate your feelings. Listen to this story of a woman who used a word picture to help her husband understand her feelings:

> At a time in our marriage when we were having a hard time, we were driving to Oregon from California and talking about whether he would continue in school. I was feeling like we couldn't continue. He was involved in a lot of ministries, had a demanding job, and was going to school. We weren't having any time together. For a large part of the drive, he said, "I have to go to

> school." Finally, somewhere in Oregon, the Lord gave me a picture I could use to help my husband understand my feelings. I said that marriage was like walking on a log and that when your marriage is healthy that log is over a low ravine. I said that right now you've got us walking over a really steep ravine. If we fall off, it's a long way down. It doesn't feel safe to me. After I finished describing this picture, he turned to me and said, "OK, I'll quit." He wasn't understanding or hearing me until I used a word picture.

Whether you use a word picture or a simpler approach to communicate your feelings, let your partner know how his or her behavior affects you emotionally.

Expectations—The final element of the SAFE skill is to *explain* your *expectations*. Communicate to your spouse what you would like to see happen. It's appropriate in this step to use phrases such as "I would appreciate it if you could..." or "Would you please...?" or "It would mean a lot to me if you could...."

The important idea here is to clearly and directly communicate your request. Notice that I say "request" and not "demand." Remember this Scripture: "A gentle answer turns away wrath, but a harsh word stirs up anger" (Proverbs 15:1). Think about it. When someone *tells* you that you must change, you'll naturally want to resist. On the other hand, when someone *asks* you to change, you are much more likely to comply. A gentle word will help your spouse respond much more productively than a harsh word. Therefore, our spouses generally respond better to a request than a demand.

Let's say that your spouse comes in at the end of every day and throws his or her dirty laundry all over the master bedroom. This behavior begins to bother you. You begin, of course, by covering for your spouse: "I understand that when you come home from work, you're anxious to get comfortable…." Continue by describing the behavior: "But when you come home and leave your clothes lying on the floor of our bedroom…." Now share your feelings: "I feel frustrated because I like a neat room." Now comes the request: "Would you please either hang up your clothes or put them in the hamper?"

Sometimes an issue is so complicated that you can't handle it by making one request. If you're having major problems in disciplining your children or if you're finding it impossible to live within a budget, you won't fix the problem with one change. In such a case, you might communicate your expectation this way: "I'd appreciate it if we could talk about this." At that point, you would have already covered for your spouse, described his or her behavior, and disclosed your feelings. Your request would be an invitation to explore the issue further.

This SAFE strategy of resolving conflict—cover sins, describe actions, disclose feelings, and explain expectations—avoids the problem of blame. When used properly, it will communicate your negative feelings in a positive way. It may also open a door of communication so that you can dialogue about the issue further.

2. *Active Listening*

One problem that many couples experience in conflict is the tendency for the discussion to escalate. One person speaks, the other interrupts. Partners fight to get their points across. Comments begin to fly without much thought. When this happens, the process resembles a sparring match, each partner giving and receiving a series of quick punches. Couples can find themselves fifteen minutes later with nothing resolved but knowing that they've been in a fight!

You can avoid the escalation of conflict through active listening. (Active listening is one of the communication tools I discussed in Chapter 5. Review those pages if you need to.) One benefit of utilizing active listening is that the whole resolution process slows down because spouses paraphrase what they hear from each other. As well, spouses will avoid misunderstandings as they communicate what they hear, giving each other opportunities to correct if necessary. Whenever you sense a conflict brewing, use this skill. This makes conflict much safer for both partners and far more productive.

Let me tell you about a time recently when I *didn't* use active listening and paid the price. I came home from a conference with a great new idea for our church. I was excited about it; I'd been thinking about something like it for months. When I described it to Naomi, I saw her frown and shake her head. She didn't think it was a good idea.

That's when I did something that blew the conversation wide open. I said to her, "Naomi, I'm immune to that frown. I know that this is the right way to go." Stupid, I know, but I was just so passionate about that idea!

Naomi and I are both even-tempered, so we didn't yell at each other, but our listening skills went out the window! Each of us tried to convince the other of our point of view. Both of us walked away hurt from the interaction.

Some time later, we talked again, and I said this to Naomi: "Honey, this thing was all my fault. I was wrong not to listen carefully to you. If I had listened to you at the beginning instead of trying to convince you, I know you would have listened to me, too. Can we start over?"

We then had a wonderful conversation that drew us closer together and opened our eyes to each other. If I had just used active listening in the first place, I could have avoided some of that pain.

3. Prayerful Negotiation

What happens if you are working through the conflict-resolution process and come to an impasse? Let's say that one of you has just used the SAFE strategy, communicating concern without blaming. Perceptively, the other of you has used active listening to track with the concerns and communicate you've heard the concerns. You're now ready to respond, but you have a problem. You don't see how you can meet your spouse's communicated expectation. You don't feel good about the request.

At this point, you as a couple need the third conflict-resolution skill: prayerful negotiation. You both want to achieve a win-win solution. Philippians 2:4 needs to shape your thinking in this case: "Each of you should look not only to your own interests, but also to the interests of others." Both interests, both perspectives, both expectations are important as partners have a problem to solve. If one of you wins and the other loses, one or both of you will probably walk away with negative feelings. In addition, distance is created in the relationship. And when this happens, no one wins.

So we must strive for win-win solutions to all our conflicts. And prayerful negotiation is the art of coming to agreement about a problem or decision that satisfies both marriage partners. Perhaps both partners won't get everything they want. But each partner will be treated fairly, and by the end of the process, both partners ought to feel good about the resolution.

When you face an impasse in the conflict-resolution process, continue with the following two steps of prayerful negotiation:

Step 1: Generate alternatives, and choose one that will satisfy both partners. If you don't want to or can't meet your partner's expectations, communicate that clearly, then begin to brainstorm together about alternatives. Think of as many ideas as you can without evaluating them. After you've created a list of all your ideas, talk about each option and see which alternative best suits both of you.

One common conflict that occurs in the first year or two of marriage is where to go for holidays such as Thanksgiving and Christmas. The conversation below illustrates how a couple might resolve such a conflict.

"Jim, it would mean a lot to me if we could spend Christmas at my parents' house. What do you think?"

"Hmm...I don't know how I feel about it. I guess I just assumed we'd spend Christmas with my folks."

"You'd rather go to your parents' house?"

"Yes, I suppose I would. It's been a tradition to open gifts and have a Christmas brunch. It would be sad to miss being with Mom and Dad."

"So it's pretty important to you?"

"I think so."

"I guess I would say that being with my family is important to me, too. I wonder if we could make some compromises?"

"We probably could. Let me get a pencil and a sheet of paper, and let's list some alternatives. I suppose we could go to my parents' house on Christmas Eve, and then we could drive to your parents' house the next morning. Maybe my family would be willing to open gifts on Christmas Eve."

"Sure. I could ask my parents about that, too."

"That's two alternatives!"

"We could spend Christmas day with each of our parents on alternate years. I'd be willing to let you go first."

"Maybe we could invite both families here?"

"That's a possibility. I'll write it down."

This husband and wife would continue to generate alternatives until they couldn't think of any more. They would then take the list and evaluate each possibility. By the end of the process, they would try to agree on one alternative that seemed best to both of them. If this happens, they've resolved their conflict. However, if they could *not* agree on an alternative that would satisfy both of them, they'd move on to Step 2.

Step 2: Take up to a week to pray about the issue, asking God to give wisdom and to change your heart. During the week, ask God to change your heart and to help you think through the issue from your spouse's point of view. "What!?" you say. "Change *my* heart?" "What about *his* heart," or "What about *her* heart?" That's just the point. You must ask God first to help *you* change. You must be open to placing your spouse's wishes first, before your own. You must ask God to help you demonstrate love to your partner. This will sometimes mean choosing to serve your spouse by changing your position.

Notice that I say *choose*. If you are manipulated or coerced into changing, that would be unhealthy for any relationship. However, *choosing* to serve your partner is healthy. Jesus serves as an example here. He said to Pilate, in essence, "You are not taking my life. I am choosing to lay it down" (John 19:10–11, paraphrase mine). The Romans didn't take Jesus' life from Him; He willingly gave it. In the same way, marriage may sometimes call upon you to willingly give up your desires and choose to lay down your life for your partner.

If you've reached this step in the conflict-resolution process, it's important that you really do pray during the week. It would be easy just to come back a week later having spent no time with God, with a heart even harder than when you began! But when you both pray about the issue, God will help you become willing to meet your partner's expectations. Such prayerful handling of the issue almost always results in some form of resolution. It brings glory to God and will actually deepen your relationship.

At the end of the week, come together for a fresh discussion, beginning your time with prayer. After prayer, share what

God has said to each of you. Then make a final decision.

If you use these three skills when you face conflict, you'll almost always find a resolution. Take a moment now and ask yourselves, is there an issue between you that would benefit from using the SAFE strategy, active listening, and/or prayerful negotiation?

Handling Anger in Conflict

Recently a young couple sat in my office for their first session of premarital counseling. They were planning to marry in three months. At one point in our session together, I asked them this question: "What fights have you had so far?" The answer to this question tells me a lot about a couple's relationship. This couple's answer was interesting.

"We don't fight. We just talk. Some of our friends say that we're not normal. They say that fighting is good because it's fun to make up!"

This attitude is common but, I think, misguided. Saying, "I love to fight because it's fun to make up" is like saying, "I love getting bashed in the face because it feels so much better when the pain subsides"! Conflict is inevitable and healthy in every marriage relationship. However, fighting is not the best way to handle conflict. The potential damage done during a fight can seriously affect the relationship.

Proverbs 20:3 provides a healthy perspective here: "It is to a man's honor to avoid strife, but every fool is quick to quarrel." Why is avoiding strife better? Because it avoids inflicting pain with hurtful words and actions. When you let loose with words and actions, you now have two issues on the table: the original conflict plus the way you've treated each other *during* the conflict. Believe me, the issues become more and more confused when this happens. It's all so unnecessary!

Fighting is generally a result of couples who do not know

how to handle their anger. Since emotional expression is not taught to us directly, we tend to simply observe others and do our best. Sadly, many people have not had healthy conflict models to observe. As these people do their best to imitate their models, they often handle their anger in a negative fashion, scuttling conflict resolution. Anger muddies the issues and makes it practically impossible to use the kinds of skills that I have described above.

You might ask, "Shouldn't I communicate my anger?" Absolutely. There is a difference, however, between *communicating* your anger and *demonstrating* your anger. Instead of communicating anger by saying, "I'm feeling angry with you right now," many couples demonstrate their anger by criticizing, yelling, or slamming doors! This boils down to nothing more than venting your anger on each other. Such venting of anger will damage the relationship.

If you find the expression of anger a problem during your conflicts, you may wish to use the following two-step strategy.[4]

A Brief Anger Strategy

1. *Admit your anger to your spouse as soon as you're aware of it.* Acknowledging your anger will tend to defuse the situation. For example, you could communicate anger in a healthy way by saying, "Honey, right now I want to admit that I'm feeling some anger about this." This statement doesn't communicate blame and is not coercive. It simply describes an emotional state. You might also say, "Would you please pray for me? I'm feeling angry right now, and I want to stay in control." You might be surprised at how disarming asking for help can be and how meaningful it is to hear your spouse pray for you.

Communicating your anger helps you stay in control and alerts your partner to help you in any way possible. It signals both partners to slow down the process and use active listening.

For many couples, communicating anger can be enough to keep the conversation moving in a positive direction.

2. *If you are in danger of venting your anger, agree to a time-out.* During conflict, one or both of you may feel that you're on the verge of venting your anger in a hurtful way. At this point, instead of pushing through the discussion, ask for a timeout. A timeout is simply agreeing to stop the conversation so that the angry person can cool off.

When using a timeout, both partners agree to separate for a time and do whatever necessary to handle the anger. This may include talking to God about your anger. It will probably mean that you think about *why* you are angry. It will certainly include looking at your partner's perspective and trying to understand it.

This process may take ten minutes for some, an hour for others, or half a day for yet others. When you begin a timeout, agree about when you will come back together to finish the discussion. Don't use a timeout to avoid the issue.

Much more might be said about handling anger. However, these two steps alone have proved helpful to many couples. If you tend to handle anger inappropriately and these two steps don't seem to help, consider seeking the assistance of a Christian counselor.

How Men and Women Handle Conflict Differently

As I researched this chapter, I talked to a number of couples about how they typically handled conflict. I received a variety of responses, of course, but a pattern did emerge. Here's what I discovered: Men and women often react to conflict differently. Listen to this husband's words:

> When I get in tense situations, I have a tendency to clam up. It worked for me for a long time before I was married! In our relationship, when we get in a tough

> situation, Sue has told me that she really needs feedback, not this silence thing. The more I'm quiet, the more it makes her crazy.

This husband's reaction is similar to many husbands all over the world! Listen to another man's thoughts: "If something is impacting me emotionally, I do better if I go away and process it, and then come back and talk. Sarah wants to talk about it now."

Psychologist John Gray describes the male's process:

> Men "process" feelings differently. They silently feel their feelings about what is bothering them, and then begin problem solving. Simply by using his right brain to problem-solve, he temporarily disengages from his feelings and automatically cools off.[5]

Do you see the pattern? Men often want to process the conflict before they speak with their wives, and women often want to handle the issue immediately. One way to visualize this tendency is to say that women have computer brains and men have file-cabinet brains! Men can simply store their problems in mental file folders and stick them in the file cabinet for the time being. Later on, they come back to extract their files and process their responses. Then they move to problem solving.

Women, on the other hand, find that the conflict computer file remains open and processes continuously. In general, women find problems difficult to shut down. The program just keeps running until they resolve their issues. Many women talk to their girlfriends to work through problems because their problems are constantly on their minds.

Wives find it difficult to understand their husbands' ability to simply set problems aside. Husbands wonder at their wives' ability to maintain intensity.

To help address this difference, husbands and wives need to be aware and sensitive to it, doing what they can to help their spouses. One wife told me recently:

> A girlfriend told me recently that she had to give her husband some time to process things. I thought, "She's right." Sometimes we expect our husbands to be on the same intensity level as we are. It's sometimes better to back off and let them have time to process it.

Wives can help their husbands by giving them time to process. That may mean asking the question, "Would you like some time to think this through before we talk?"

Husbands can help their wives by not clamming up. Husbands, if you need time to think, you can simply say, "Honey, I would like to talk about this, but I want to ask you to give me time to think it through. Can we discuss this tomorrow morning right after breakfast?" This type of statement helps reduce your wife's anxiety by letting her know that you aren't just withdrawing from her.

As a couple, do you need to employ one or more of the suggested strategies for handling your anger when conflict arises? Take a moment to discuss how you can handle anger in a healthy fashion. (If you'd like some additional ideas, read Appendix C, "Successful Couples' Top Ten Rules for Handling Conflict Fairly" on page 187.)

Exercise 1: Talking About Our Style

Each of you answer the following questions or complete the statements as indicated. Listen carefully to each other and discuss the material as openly as possible.

1. Check one of the statements below:

_____I tend to avoid conflict. (If so, can you say why?)

_____I try to handle the issue, but usually wind up making a mess of things. (After reading this chapter, do you have some idea why?)

_____I do fairly well with many elements of the conflict-resolution process. (Great! Can you say which areas are difficult for you?)

_____I am totally comfortable with these skills. I'm able to share my negative feelings in a positive way and process conflict well almost all of the time.

2. We tend to experience the most conflict about…

_____Work-related issues: time spent at work; whether it intrudes on our marriage relationship.

_____In-laws: the way they impact our relationship.

_____Sexual relationship: our level of satisfaction.

_____Communication: the way we speak, listen, and share our lives emotionally.

_____Spiritual partnership: the way we share our spiritual lives.

_____Acceptance of differences: how we respond to our differences.

_____Finances: the way we earn, save, and spend money.

_____Parenting: agreeing on and following through with a game plan for discipline.

_____Other:

3. One strength I observe about your ability to resolve conflict is….

4. One area in which you could grow to better resolve conflict is….

5. One mutual change that would help us resolve conflict is…

Now is a great time to pray together briefly, asking God to help you in this area of your marriage. Commit any decisions to Him and ask for help in the days to come.

Exercise 2: The SAFE Strategy

Use the SAFE strategy I've described in this chapter to talk about a negative issue in your relationship without conveying blame. Remember the sequence:

Sins—cover
Actions—describe
Feelings—disclose
Expectations—explain

The key phrases are:
S: "I know..." or "I understand...."
A: "When you..." or "When I see you...."
F: "I feel..." or "I'm feeling...."
E: "I would appreciate..." or "Would you please...?"

Each of you take a turn beginning a discussion using the SAFE strategy.

Now turn to Appendix B, "Our Commitment to Marriage Enrichment" (page 184) and, in the space provided, jot down insights you've gained from this chapter and changes you could make to further enrich your marriage.

Chapter Seven

Foundation 4: Vital Spiritual Friendship

Couples with healthy marriages have at least one characteristic in common: Spouses share their lives with each other. On many levels, spouses in a vital marriage grow closer and closer together, bringing down emotional walls and building emotional, physical, and spiritual bonds. In such a marriage, partners are each other's best friends.

Nowhere is this friendship more satisfying or more important than in a couple's spiritual life. James Dobson received a letter from a woman after her husband had left her. The letter eloquently reminds us of the importance of marriage spirituality. Listen to this woman's words:

> My husband recently left me after fifteen years of marriage. We had a great physical, emotional, and intellectual relationship. But something was missing...we had no spiritual bond between us. Please tell young couples that...a good marriage must have its foundation in Him in order to experience lasting love, peace, and joy.[1]

Pause for a moment and ask yourselves these questions: Are we spiritual friends? Can we talk about our spiritual lives with each other? Can we discuss the Scriptures? Is prayer a regular part of our relationship? Can we minister together, sharing a common goal of service? Do we feel spiritually connected with each other?

Couples sometimes feel confused about how their spiritual lives should fit together. They're uncertain about what spiritual friendship actually means. I did a radio interview recently to talk about the benefits of couples praying together. The radio interviewer was polite and interested, but he confessed to me over the air, "My wife and I have a good relationship, but frankly, we pray very little together. How do you explain that?"

My explanation was simple. Spiritual friendship is needed for Christian couples to experience the deepest levels of intimacy. It's not so much a question of "How close are we now?" but "How much closer *could we be* if we shared a spiritual friendship?" This interviewer's *good* relationship with his wife might have been *great* had this element been operating in his marriage.

No matter where your marriage relationship stands right now, whether warmly relational or routinely functional, "couple prayer" and other elements of a spiritual friendship will enrich your marriage. In fact, if you want to attain the deepest level of marriage, you must incorporate this element into your relationship. It is foundational for a healthy, growing marriage. Spiritual friendship provides positives in marriage that no other element of the marital foundation can provide. Since you are interested in marital enrichment, this area represents fertile ground in your search for a closer relationship.

What Is Spiritual Friendship?

Spiritual friendship has two elements: (1) developing your relationship with God *as a couple* through activities such as couple prayer or Bible study; and (2) sharing your *individual* spiritual lives with each other through ongoing dialogue about your beliefs, your faith, and your individual relationships with God. Essentially, these two elements mean sharing your lives in Christ. The development of spiritual intimacy is *interactional.* You interact as you share your beliefs or talk about what God is doing in your life; you interact as you pray together; you interact as you serve others together.

But spiritual friendship is more than just sharing certain spiritual activities. It's possible to pray together, for example, and remain distant spiritually. Spiritual intimacy demands a gradual lowering of protective barriers; spouses must invite each other into what was once a totally private area of their lives. Norm Wright has written that spiritual intimacy involves "a willingness to overcome your sense of discomfort over sharing spiritually and learn to see your marriage together as a spiritual adventure."[2] He rightly observes that developing a spiritual friendship means a willing attitude: a desire to create the emotional safety, open communication, and trust that this dimension of your relationship requires.

Ecclesiastes 4:12 contains an appropriate metaphor for this shared spiritual friendship: "Though one may be overpowered, two can defend themselves. A cord of three strands is not quickly broken." In my previous book *Praying With the One You Love,* I wrote these words about this Bible verse:

> In the ancient world, a rope was formed and strengthened as individual strands were twisted together. In the same way, couples who invite the Lord into their relationship...find their lives uniquely interwoven. Each strand—husband, wife, and God Himself—combines with the others to form a strong cord that will withstand the many forces that can unravel a marriage relationship.[3]

A couple forms a three-way friendship when they invite Christ into their relationship. What a powerful and dynamic means of deepening your relationship with God and with each other!

Paul Stevens makes an apt observation about spirituality:

> Disciplines are not paths of spiritual accomplishment by which human beings reach God. Rather, they are ways of breaking down the barriers which keep us from being found by the seeking Father.[4]

When a husband and wife develop a spiritual friendship, they work together to break down those barriers. When that happens, they find that God is a vital part of their couple friendship. Whether through couple prayer, guided conversation around spiritual issues, sharing in the partnership of service, or other spiritual disciplines, walls come down between husband and wife and between the couple and their Father. What could be more satisfying, more significant, or more challenging?

Roadblocks to Spiritual Friendship

Of course, if you seek to develop a spiritual friendship with each other, you'll face roadblocks along the way. Anything as priceless as a Christ-centered relationship could not possibly come easily! In fact, friendship of any kind develops only with commitment, time, and effort. Spouses serious about developing their spiritual friendship must become intentional about it. Obstacles can be overcome—the prize is worth it—but only when couples see the value of such a friendship and make choices to move in that direction.

What follows is a list of roadblocks you'll have to intentionally move past as you strive for a spiritual friendship with each other.

Time

Couples mention time as the biggest difficulty in developing the spiritual aspect of their relationships. Couples today are busy. In many families, both husband and wife work. The demands of home, work, church, and marriage can seem almost overwhelming—too much to do in too little time. Spiritual disciplines such as couple prayer and Bible reading often fall low on the priority list in such pressure-packed days.

But if we all took a good look at our schedules, we'd realize that we all have some discretionary time. And on some level, we all make choices about how to spend that time. If your spiritual partnership is important to you, you'll have to intentionally set aside some of your discretionary time to develop couple prayer and other activities that will strengthen your spiritual friendship. It's a matter of making a priority of the spiritual aspect of your relationship.

One attitude that tends to kill motivation is an all-or-nothing mentality. This kind of attitude says, "If we can't pray together all we want to, we will not pray at all; if we can't connect spiritually every day, we'll forget this aspect of our relationship." Don't let this kind of attitude set you up for failure. Instead, use the time you *do* have as effectively as you can. Make "couple spirituality" a priority but realize that something is better than nothing. As you develop this area, you'll be able to increase the time you spend together and see the benefits slowly mount up.

Remember, too, that couples must live integrated lives. God understands that you have laundry to do, meals to prepare, and children to care for. These activities are a part of life, not distractions to resent. Our Father joins us in every area of our lives, not just in prayer or at church. Don't feel guilty about what you *aren't* doing; feel good about what you *are* doing to develop your spiritual friendship.

Having said all of that, couples who wish to develop their spiritual friendship must make commitments. Statements such as "Let's meet on Mondays and Fridays at 7 A.M. to pray together" signify such a commitment. No part of life, after all, thrives without attention. Committing to your spiritual friendship may mean arranging for the children's needs; unplugging the phone; and simply making prayer, Bible study, and individual sharing happen.

Fear of Intimacy

Fear of intimacy is another roadblock you may face as you seek to grow closer spiritually. Spiritual intimacy can be scary! It requires that spouses disclose who they are and what's going on inside of them. Conversations about where you are spiritually, for example, require that you share thoughts and emotions about your personal relationship with God. If in couple prayer, I share my feelings with God, I am also sharing my feelings with my spouse! Spiritual friendship often transports us to the most fertile ground of marital intimacy.

Do you face this roadblock to spiritual depth in your relationship? If so, you can overcome this fear by talking it through with each other. One of you might need to say, "I'm afraid you won't accept me if I'm real with you." If you feel this way, then *say* it. I remember a young husband who finally mustered up enough courage to say this to his wife in my office. His wife's positive response completely astonished him. What your partner wants is *you*! He or she will support you if you reveal your true self. Acceptance is almost always the result of such honest sharing. Couples who commit themselves to taking the risks of spiritual friendship reap the extraordinary benefits. It may not always feel comfortable, but the risk is worth it!

Conflict

The third roadblock to developing spiritual friendship is conflict. As I said in Chapter 6, all couples experience conflict. When problems remain unresolved, the friction can decrease a couple's motivation to pursue spiritual friendship.

One bit of counsel regarding this obstacle: Allow yourselves to be "in process." No couple is totally together at all times. If you wait until perfection reigns in your marriage to develop your couple spirituality, you'll never begin! If you'd like to develop spiritual friendship but know you have some issues, begin the process of spiritual friendship by candidly expressing your concerns to each other. Agree to do what you can do, even though tension sometimes exists. Believe me, developing this part of your relationship will impact unresolved conflict!

You *can* overcome all the obstacles to spiritual friendship. With God's help, you can break through and experience spiritual intimacy as a couple. As you do, you'll find the following three disciplines key in the development of your spiritual friendship.

1. Couple Prayer

Couple prayer is the centerpiece of couple spirituality. If spouses want to develop a spiritual friendship with each other and with God, if they desire to make Christ the center of their relationship, they must make couple prayer a priority. James Dobson has concluded the following about couple prayer: "A meaningful prayer life is essential in maintaining a Christ-centered home."[5]

For all couples, the ongoing discipline of joining together in prayer can make a difference in your relationship to each other and to God.

The Benefits of Couple Prayer

In over twenty years of marriage to my wife, Naomi, couple prayer has flooded our relationship with the warm glow of God's presence. We have experienced the incredible benefits of a joint prayer life. Our prayer times together have contributed something unique to our relationship and have deepened our love for each other. The benefits below suggest just a few of the ways couple prayer has been so positive in our relationship. You can enjoy these benefits, too!

First, couple prayer promotes intimacy. Earlier in this book, I discussed how spouses can foster relational intimacy in their marriage. Spouses must reveal who they are to each other, offering understanding and acceptance to each other as they self-disclose. When partners pray together, truly seeking God as a couple, they are in fact revealing themselves to God *and* to each other! When I hear Naomi pray, "Father, I'm concerned about my schedule next week" or "Lord, I want to love you more," I learn more about her. Such self-disclosure helps me to know her better. When spouses pray together, week after week, year in and year out, they gain a picture of each other's hearts. They cannot help but grow closer to each other.

Listen to what one young woman said after she and her husband finally decided to begin praying together:

> I never dreamed what has happened in our marriage during the past year was possible. We've gone along for years just sort of ho-hum. Nothing bad, nothing spectacular—just steady...I can't explain why or what happened, but there is this incredible sense of bonding or closeness now that we never had before. Sometimes I call him and pray a sentence prayer for him over the phone. He does the same....Others have seen our relationship change.[6]

That "incredible sense of bonding or closeness" is a common testimony for those who make couple prayer a regular part of their lives. One husband told me simply, "Bottom line: Couple prayer improves our relationship."

Second, praying together helps couples face difficulties. Crises, tragedies, and transitions of all kinds will happen in every marriage. I can promise you that! Praying together can make a difference in helping couples weather such difficulties.

Perhaps you've known a couple who experienced a crisis or difficulty in their lives: perhaps a financial crisis or the loss of a loved one. Instead of moving through it together, they backed away from each other and became more distant.

That doesn't have to happen! Couple prayer can be the cement that holds couples together during trying times. When we pray together during tough times, we remember our dependence upon God. Even Jesus said, "By myself I can do nothing" (John 5:30). When Martin Luther prayed, he would sometimes refer to himself as an "empty vessel" needing to be filled. Every believer can resonate with such feelings. Spouses must know that without the active involvement of God in their lives and family, they will not experience God's best. They are dependent as a couple upon Him.

Remember Jesus said, "For where two or three come together in my name, there am I with them" (Matthew 18:20). When partners pray together, they invite God's presence into their lives. They express their need for Him to do whatever is necessary to take care of the issue. Relying on God takes away the temptation to blame each other or become overly anxious. It helps a couple face the difficulty together, knowing that God is in charge.

Listen to this observation:

> To weather the crises of life, couples must understand that they are dependent upon God, that he is their

> Source. Peace comes as we look to God for our answers. Together, we invite God into the circumstances of our lives. This sense of dependency allows us to rest in the arms of our Father, rather than pull away from our spouse when the tough times of life intrude.[7]

When partners establish a prayer life together, life's difficulties only serve to unify them as they go together into God's presence. Praying together strengthens the harmony and unity within a couple's marriage.

Third, couple prayer helps prevent sustained anger in the relationship. As mentioned in the last chapter, you will feel angry with each other sometimes. One of you will feel irritated that the other didn't do the laundry or finish cleaning the garage. Of course, more serious offenses are also a part of every marriage relationship. When one or both of you feel angry, one of the most destructive things you can do is hold on to your anger. As you do so, your anger can grow and fester, possibly turning into bitterness. If this happens on multiple issues, a relationship can be flooded with accumulated offenses.

Couple prayer helps prevent such sustained anger. Remember that Jesus gave this command to all believers:

> If you are offering your gift at the altar and there remember that your brother has something against you, leave your gift there in front of the altar. First go and be reconciled to your brother; then come and offer your gift (Matthew 5:23–24).

When spouses pray together regularly, they find it extremely difficult to hang on to offenses or to keep the fires of anger ignited. Every time you pray with your spouse, these questions naturally come to mind: Is there something between us as a couple? Do I need to forgive my spouse or discuss an issue with him or her before we pray? It's hard to enter into the presence of a holy God when you're maintaining a hard heart toward your spouse! For that reason, couples who pray together find themselves more motivated to resolve their conflicts and to release their anger appropriately.

How Do Couples Pray Together?

At this point, you may be sold on the need for integrating couple prayer into your relationship. But you may also be thinking, "We don't know how to pray together. We want to begin but need some help." Or "We've tried praying together before but haven't been able to sustain it." If so, I recommend my book *Praying With the One You Love.* It will help you on a number of practical levels to help you start and sustain couple prayer. The suggestions that follow are based on the information in that book.

Develop a basic structure for prayer. Sometimes couples want to pray together but don't know how to start a prayer time or how to keep it going. These couples need some structure. Different patterns of prayer work for different couples. Some have used a simple pattern that suggests four themes of prayer using the acrostic A–C–T–S. The letters stand for *Adoration, Confession, Thanksgiving,* and *Supplication* (requests).

Naomi and I use a system in which we visualize prayer "laps." To "run a lap" is to complete a certain theme in prayer. We complete one theme in prayer before moving to the next one. The basic themes that we pray through are described below.

In Matthew 6:9 Jesus emphasizes *praise* as the way to begin prayer: "Our Father in heaven, hallowed be your name." This is a statement of praise! Couples can profitably begin their times of prayer together by spending a few moments praising God.

This means recognizing God for who He is and thanking Him for what He has done. Naomi and I always begin our prayer time this way. To do this, we sometimes sing a chorus or read a Psalm of thanksgiving. This helps us set our focus on the Lord.

When finished with this theme, couples can move to *intercession*: praying for others. Matthew 6:10 says this: "Your kingdom come, your will be done on earth as it is in heaven." Think of the word "kingdom" here as God's rule and authority. In this passage, Jesus encourages us to invite God's kingdom to rule! Pray for God's will to be accomplished and His kingdom to come crashing into the situations around you, into the lives of those you know.

When Naomi and I come to this theme in our prayer time, we pray for our family, our church, our friends, and our nation. Allow God to lead you to the areas that need your intercession each day. You may want to keep a prayer notebook to help you remember needs.

Our next lap is *petition,* a time for us to pray for our own needs. In Matthew 6:11 Jesus prays, "Give us today our daily bread." This is a statement of dependence upon God. Following Christ's example, Naomi and I bring our needs to God. Sometimes before we pray I will ask her, "Is there something I can pray for you about today?" At other times, we are completely spontaneous. We also pray for our needs as a couple, including issues that affect us both. We might pray, for example, for wisdom concerning a decision we need to make. We have learned that we can bring anything to God, and over the years, we have done exactly that.

At some point in the prayer time, we also pause to *confess our sins* and release others who have sinned against us. "Forgive us our debts, as we also have forgiven our debtors" (Matthew 6.12), the Scripture says. This involves asking God to help you recognize any knots of anger you have toward others and then helping you release the people involved. Secondly, it means to confess sin in your own lives that may keep you from intimacy with God.

Couples can understandably feel awkward about confession. As you seek to pray together in this way, be sensitive to the level of transparency that you have achieved in your relationship. Even partners who have a close marriage might best leave some things between themselves and God. If this is a problem during a prayer time, simply say, "Let's pause here and speak to God silently." Then resume praying together when you have finished that element of prayer.

I talk about other elements of prayer in *Praying With the One You Love*. However, these are the basic ones: praise, intercession, petition, and confession. Remember above all things that prayer is friendship with God. Prayer is the means by which we stay in loving contact with our Father. Regular prayer deepens our relationship to Him and to each other. It is the foundational pillar of a spiritual friendship in marriage.

The key to developing this area in your marriage is to have regular prayer times. Every couple will vary here, according to the season of their marriage and the schedules they keep. However, regular prayer times together make all the difference in your spiritual friendship. The best way to make prayer a regular part of your life is to *plan* it.

If you are just starting, plan a ten- or fifteen-minute prayer time, twice a week. As you get used to praying together, increase the time and frequency. Maybe even take a moment right now to talk about your schedules and how you can make prayer a part of your life together.

2. Spiritual Conversation

Any kind of true intimacy—emotional, intellectual, or sexual—involves honest sharing and deep communication. Spiritual intimacy is no different. Spouses who successfully develop their spiritual friendship do so by sharing their spiritual journeys with each other.

Such conversation presents a unique window into each other's lives. You each expose your soul to the other through self-disclosure and listening. This back-and-forth sharing of spiritual friendship cannot help but strengthen every other facet of your marriage relationship. In addition, it actually spurs each of you on, promoting spiritual growth.

Naomi and I talk about our lives in Christ regularly and in a variety of ways. Not long ago, we talked about the pressure I feel to perform well. The discussion began with a simple question: "How are you doing?"

Instead of hiding my feelings, I decided to talk about them.

"I'm feeling let down, like I didn't do the job I needed to. I'm wondering how pleased God is with me."

This discussion led us to talk about my childhood and about my boyhood relationship with my father. As we talked, the discussion turned to what we both believe about God's love—how His expectations differ from that inner voice inside of me that says I'm no good unless I perform perfectly.

Naomi listened carefully, helping me to know myself a bit better. We've had this discussion before, and this time we came away understanding each other better, having listened to each other's spiritual journey and having experienced God's love together.

Many couples develop their spiritual friendship by simply discussing their current spiritual condition, answering the questions, "Where am I spiritually?" and "What has God said to me recently?" Paul Stevens says that this kind of spiritual friendship "is where persons have become pilgrims together, taking off layers of masks and getting to transparency."[8] This kind of conversation reveals spouses' hearts and sometimes leads them directly to couple prayer as they become aware of a need or an opportunity for thanksgiving.

Beyond such sharing, partners can discuss Scripture together, share their beliefs, talk about their feelings as they serve Christ together, and discuss shared spiritual experiences such as worship or prayer. They may discuss their spiritual history or how they came to believe what they believe. The sharing of a couple's spiritual journey happens in all these ways, and more.

Listen to my friend Angus McDonald describe the spiritual friendship he enjoys with his wife, Connie:

> When we're on car trips, one of the things we talk about is what's outside the car window. Look at that mountain. Look at the sunset. We spend a lot of time enjoying nature together. We do that in our spiritual journey, too. Look at what God is doing in our lives here, we say. The landscape changes as you go along. The things that were prominent in the spiritual landscape change at a later time in your life. New truths are always emerging to consider; new things that you are learning. New perspectives that God is bringing. Connie and I spend a lot of time discussing the spiritual landscape around us.

Do you sense the excitement of this couple's spiritual journey? The "spiritual landscape" includes so much! Imagine the benefits of sharing this journey together. The key is becoming aware of your spirituality—your connectedness with God—and being willing to open your spiritual self with each other. Such spiritual self-disclosure, together with a willingness and interest in hearing each other's unique spiritual perspective, will help insure a shared spiritual journey.

Perhaps take a moment even now to take another step down that path. What spiritual conversation can you have right now? Maybe it can start with asking each other a simple question such as "What has God done in your life recently?"

3. Service

Kurt and Lynn are a couple in their early thirties. They taught Sunday school together for two years, leading a young marrieds class. When the Sunday school coordinator asked each of them to take a separate class to fill some vacancies, they both said "yes." It was a chance to serve, they thought, and perhaps expand their ministry. Listen to Lynn's words a year later:

> Our shared ministry was bumpy at first. We had to learn to work together, but after several months we realized how powerful it was to serve together. We had an equal burden for the class and could talk and pray about what was needed. When we split up, it took us in different directions. We decided that we wouldn't do separate classes again. The closeness we feel when we serve together is just so great.

What is so powerful about serving Christ together? One wife said simply, "Most of what we have done in ministry in our married life has been together, and so we have had the same focus." When couples move in the same direction, concentrating their conversation and prayer times around their common service, they experience the focus of united purpose.

When you serve as a couple, you can enjoy the benefits of shared ministry such as the connectedness and synergism that happens with a shared purpose. When spouses cooperate together they often increase the effect that either one of them could have had alone. The spiritual gifts and motivations of both partners are utilized together and find a greater expression than either one could have separately.

One wife told me, "When we say 'yes' to ministry, we always ask, 'Is this going to divide us?' There's a lot of strength in couple power!" I know a couple who work together as volunteers in Young Life. Since the husband owns his own business, he puts in long hours. If he and his wife also chose separate areas of ministry, they'd experience further fragmentation of their lives. Instead, their work together in Young Life unifies their hearts while releasing both partners' skills, gifts, and talents into this important ministry.

Aquila and Priscilla provide a wonderful picture of spiritual friendship in marriage. We see them teaching and serving side by side in Acts 18:1–4, 18–26. When Paul sends greetings to them in the Epistles, he always mentions them together. Aquila and Priscilla are a team. They work together in harmony. We can well imagine the obstacles they had to overcome, but we also see the positive example of a shared ministry focus.

Am I saying that partners should never take on ministry without each other? Of course not. I do recommend, however, that couples have some area of common service. And when partners do serve in separate areas, they need to talk and pray about these areas together.

Spiritual friendship is so important. I encourage you to pursue it in all of the ways I've listed above. To help you build the spiritual aspect of your marriage, I've provided exercises below. Choose the one that reflects your current need. If you have time, you may wish to do all three!

Exercise 1: Spiritual Conversation[9]

I've designed the following questions to help you share your spiritual journey together. Take turns talking and listening. Go through as many questions and complete as many statements as are profitable for you. Please consider these questions and statements as starting points only; explore other related issues as they arise.

1. When was the first time you realized that God loves you? Share one or two of the major spiritual growth points in your life since then.

2. What are you currently doing to stay close to God? What disciplines help you draw near to the Father? What hinders you from having an even deeper relationship with God?

3. Are you content right now? If not, what are the major areas that produce feelings of discontentment? How does discontentment affect your relationship with God?

4. Who (apart from each other) is your most important friend? What does that person add to your life? How does he or she help your relationship to God?

5. What most often makes you feel guilty? How do you handle that guilt? Does guilt hinder your life or cause you to draw closer to God?

6. Something I've wanted to tell you about my spiritual life is....

Exercise 2: Couple Prayer

1. How would you describe our prayer life together? Would you like it to be different? Is couple prayer a priority for us? Why or why not?

2. What could we do to improve our couple prayer life? How can we make prayer a regular part of our relationship?

Now, why not spend about ten minutes praying together? Begin by spending time praising God, then follow with prayer for yourselves, then for others.

Exercise 3: Talking About Service[10]

Discuss the questions below based on your need.

If you are already serving together, complete these sentences:

1. The area(s) I most enjoy serving with you is (are)....
2. The gifts and talents that you bring to our joint ministry are....
3. One problem that shared ministry presents to our marriage relationship is....

If you want to develop service together:

1. God often uses you to touch others in the following ways....
2. The ways that I would like to minister with you are....
3. If we served together, we'd have to watch out for the following issues....

Now turn to Appendix B, "Our Commitment to Marriage Enrichment" (page 184) and, in the space provided, jot down insights you've gained from this chapter and changes you could make to further enrich your marriage.

Part Three

Going Even Deeper

Chapter Eight

Deepening Your Emotional Bond

As you read this chapter, you may still be on your weekend away. That's great! This is a positive chapter that will help you move closer together as a couple—perfect for your time away. On the other hand, you may have already finished your weekend together and have decided to complete this chapter at a later time, continuing your marriage enrichment beyond the weekend. You can use both Chapters 8 and 9 in either of these ways.

Your Emotional Bond

Recently, Joe and Kathy sat in my office asking for help. Married for four years, they had a solid relationship, yet they came with a problem.

Kathy began by assuring me, "We're married for good. There's no question about that."

"Great beginning," I thought.

Joe went on, "The problem is that we think we've lost something. We don't know what to do about it."

I waited, wondering where they were going.

Finally, Kathy explained. "The problem is...well, there just isn't much electricity between us any more. There's no romance. We're wondering how we get it back."

I sat back in my chair and let out a sigh. I'd heard several couples tell me the same thing over the years. A number of factors come into play to drain the sense of excitement in a marriage: physical exhaustion, familiarity, the burdens of heavy responsibilities and time commitments. More than these problems, it seems as if some spouses simply lose their way. They forget the priority of their relationship. Husbands especially tend to say, "Been there, done that. Now it's time to move on to real life," as if such intense feelings must be consigned to a time before marriage!

As I listened to this couple, I also felt relief. They had just described an area in which they could grow! Something could be done about it. In fact, *any* couple can make changes that will help regain the excitement of married love. This couple did, in fact, begin to enjoy once again the "electricity" by working on the elements contained in this chapter.

Couples interested in marriage enrichment want to experience feelings of warmth, excitement, and closeness. In fact, successful couples will tell you that these feelings are an important part of their marriages. How do these feelings become a part of your marriage? In addition to the concepts we've already discussed in this book, couples mention ideas such as these: "Be best friends"; "Make your partner feel loved every day"; "Build up your partner"; "Don't let the romance go out of your marriage."

As I've pondered these kinds of comments, I've noticed one common thread. All of these activities help partners establish and maintain a close bond between each other. Dr. Henry Cloud, a clinical psychologist and author, explains the meaning of the word "bond": "*Bonding* is the ability to establish an emotional attachment to another person. It's the ability to relate to another on the deepest level."[1] Simply put, to bond to each other is to form an emotional attachment with each other. Successful spouses know how to deepen the emotional attachment between each other and make their marriage a progressively more satisfying one.

We can explain bonding in another way. Any time a husband and wife have a positive interaction, they generate warmth between them. When these interactions happen over and over again, in a variety of ways, both spouses feel cared for, and these shared experiences deepen the relationship. Together, they build the framework of emotional bonding little by little over a long period of time with each positive experience. In the best marriages, this process never stops.

Of course, God planned it this way! He didn't create us to live in isolation but in loving relationships with others. Thus the apostle John said, "Let us love one another, for love comes from God. Everyone who loves has been born of God and knows God" (1 John 4:7). Beyond this general command to pursue love, Paul directs husbands to "treasure" their wives (Ephesians 5:25). In fact, we can translate the original language of this verse as "keep on treasuring your wives." And wives must reciprocate. Marriage partners must never stop treasuring each other.

Obviously, the foundational elements we have discussed earlier in this book—commitment, communicating, resolving conflicts in healthy ways, spiritual friendship—contribute to this process of bonding. Along with these elements, three additional and related components also deepen the emotional bond couples feel toward each other. These are, in fact, the elements that I shared with Joe and Kathy:

1. caring,
2. romancing, and
3. befriending.

Let me describe each of these in more detail.

1. Caring

When spouses say and do things to please their partners, they demonstrate caring for each other. Such caring may be as simple as a pleasant smile or as elaborate as a thoughtful surprise. A small gift, a warm "thank you," a compliment, or a hug might all indicate caring. When a husband and wife commonly display such caring behavior in their marriage, they deepen the emotional bond between them. Each caring act generates a spark of warmth that makes the marriage better.

One biblical word for such acts of caring is *"blessing."* In the Old Testament, to bless someone meant to speak a word of power that imparted a tangible benefit to that person. In the New Testament, the word most often meant to speak well of someone. In His Word, God commands us to speak blessing to those around us (Romans 12:14 NIV; James 3:10 NASB). This blessing must begin with our marriage partners!

Let me give you an appropriate image for what happens when spouses invest such caring behavior in each other. We can describe a couple's caring interactions as deposits in an Emotional Bank Account.[2] Whenever one partner speaks a kind word or offers a caring behavior to the other, he or she makes a deposit in this Emotional Bank Account. Kindness, courtesy, thoughtfulness—any caring behavior—will increase the balance in the account.

Spouses can make withdrawals as well. A minor disagreement or an angry comment would definitely drain the account. But don't worry. Every marriage will experience some of those withdrawals. The key is to ensure that you always have a large balance in your Emotional Bank Account so that your deposits far outweigh your withdrawals.

In successful marriages, husbands and wives keep each other's Emotional Bank Accounts full. They constantly make deposits! They exhibit caring behaviors all the time, and that means they foster emotional bonding daily. They nurture relational warmth that deepens emotional attachment. That emotional bond is good for any marriage.

One last thought to remember: Caring words and behaviors are simply expressions of love. John Powell defines married love as the "basic attitude of concern for the satisfaction, security, and development of the one loved."[3] Caring behaviors demonstrate this attitude of concern and as a result deeply satisfy each marriage partner. The couple I mentioned at the beginning of this chapter, Joe and Kathy, had lost part of this attitude of concern. Small acts of caring had diminished. As a result, feelings of warmth diminished as well.

Caring With Your Words

You can demonstrate caring in a variety of ways; you can start by showing caring in your words to each other. The Bible offers a powerful command about the kinds of words we need to speak to one another: "Do not let any unwholesome talk come out of your mouths, but only what is helpful for building others up according to their needs, that it may benefit those who listen" (Ephesians 4:29). Caring words build up your marriage partner. As caring words benefit your spouse, they also do wonders for your relationship.

A quick way to get a handle on caring words is to think of the "Four As": approval, affection, acceptance, and appreciation. When you speak these kinds of words, you not only build up each other, you establish an emotional bond between you!

Words of *approval* attribute value to each other. When you use them, you recognize each other's strengths and assets as well as each other's efforts to improve. Approving words communicate these messages: "You're a capable person"; "You do this very well"; "You are really making progress." Approval encourages you and your marriage partner to excel in the race of life. Frequent compliments will mean the world to you both!

Words of *affection* add the dimension of tenderness and passion to your marriage. They demonstrate your delight in and caring for each other. Affectionate words communicate these messages: "You're desirable"; "I'm drawn to you"; "I have deep feelings of love for you." Naomi and I were with a couple recently when the husband said to his wife, "You have such a wonderful smile." It communicated volumes about the deep affection this man had for his wife.

Words of *acceptance* help you both feel secure. Accepting words communicate these messages: "I'm for you no matter what"; "I understand your weaknesses and love you in spite of them;" "You don't have to win my love with your performance." How important such words are! I apologized to Naomi recently for forgetting something she had asked me to pick up at the store. This happens frequently—I sometimes have my mind elsewhere! I told her, "I'm sorry I'm so forgetful of details." And Naomi replied, "That's OK. You have a lot of other great qualities." What a communication of acceptance!

Words of *appreciation* introduce the aspect of gratefulness into your marriage. Think for a moment about how you feel when someone thanks you. It feels great, doesn't it? Appreciative words communicate these messages: "I'm grateful for what you do and who you are"; "I'm aware of your great qualities"; "I'm thankful for you." Words of appreciation help you both feel wanted and needed. These words spur both of you on to continue doing things that build the relationship.

Joe and Kathy had forgotten how important caring words were. They forgot how they could build each other up through such messages. As Joe and Kathy became aware again of how to bless each other with caring words, their relationship began to change. Emotional warmth began to grow again.

Caring With Your Actions

You can also express caring for each other in what you *do*. Dr. Ross Campbell suggests that children need concrete demonstrations of love from their parents so that they can *feel* the love that their parents have for them. He further suggests that focused attention, positive eye contact, and loving touch all communicate love in a tangible way that children can understand.[4] I believe that Dr. Campbell's ideas work just as well between husband and wife as they do between parent and child. We all need such tangible demonstrations of love. When you tangibly show love to each other, you generate warmth between each other and deepen the emotional bond you feel toward each other.

Let's consider each of Dr. Campbell's ideas in more depth. *Focused attention* is the simple act of giving time to your spouse by completely focusing on him or her. The television, the newspaper, the computer, the kids, the telephone—*everything* else—take a back seat to the one you love. I suggest that two great times to focus attention on each other is whenever you leave each other and when you first see each other again. As small as this seems, spouses I've spoken with have repeatedly mentioned their appreciation for this kind of attention.

When you wake up, say, "Good morning" and give each other a kiss or hug. When you leave for work, say how much you'll miss each other or simply give each other a warm "goodbye" and a brief touch. When you arrive home for the day, smile and say "hello." Tell each other about the events of your day and listen carefully to what the other has to say. When you go to bed, say, "Good night" and give each other a kiss. Focus your attention on each other at these crucial times. These behaviors communicate caring in concrete ways that both of you can understand.

Positive eye contact is also a tangible way of saying, "I care." Remember how you used to look lovingly at each other before you were married? You'd share a look of love with each other in a crowded room or before leaving each other for the night. Over the years, couples can begin to lose this simple act of caring. Before they realize it, spouses can begin to hardly look at each other!

Give each other warm, positive eye contact when speaking to each other. A positive act of caring that will generate warmth between you is to simply catch each other's eyes and smile. Make this happen twice a day. No words, just eye contact and a smile. How simple! But how warmly relational.

Loving touch is another powerful way of communicating blessing to each other. It says loud and clear, "I care for you! I love you!" Listen to Ed Wheat's words about touch:

> A tender touch tells us that we are cared for. It can calm our fears, soothe pain, bring us comfort, or give us the blessed satisfaction of emotional security. As adults, touching continues to be a primary means of communicating with those we love.[5]

I'm talking about what is often called "nondemand touching." It's touch that is not sexual nor a prelude to sex. This kind of touching includes snuggling, cuddling, sleeping close to each other, hugging, and holding hands. It might be as simple as placing your hand on your spouse's shoulder. However you choose to lovingly touch each other, this kind of interaction communicates warmth and caring. Through it, you reassure each other that you are there for each other.

Caring behaviors might include so much more. Any time you reach out in a tangible way for each other's satisfaction, security, and development, you build an emotional bond between you.

2. Romancing

I have already written that committed love is one of the foundational pillars of a great marriage. This kind of love is based on the marital promises and the choices we make to fulfill those promises. However, committed love does not preclude romantic love. In fact, most couples I know want the excitement, the warmth, and the emotion of romance to operate in their marriages. Romance is an important part of the emotional bonding I discussed earlier.

Recently, I spoke to a group of couples about the element of romance in their marriages. I had known each couple personally for many years, and every one of them exhibited a close, dynamic marriage. The chemistry between partners was obvious, their passion demonstrated in many different ways.

I asked these couples how they maintained the romance in their marriages. How could they have such deep feelings of passion after so many years? Each couple had the same answer: "We work at it."

Surprised? Did you think that romance should be a spontaneous expression of passion and excitement? Sometimes it might be. But like everything else in marriage, romance requires thought and action.

Dr. Ed Wheat gives one of the best definitions of romantic love that I've ever read. He says that romantic love is "a pleasurable learned response to the way your partner looks and feels, to the things your partner says and does, and to the emotional experiences you share."[6] Dr. Wheat points out that romantic love is a *learned* response. It has to do with your thoughts about each other, how you choose to respond to each other, and the way you shape your time together.

Romantic love is *not* infatuation. Infatuation centers on fantasy or novelty, and someone who is infatuated is often out of control and focused more on him- or herself than on the object of the infatuation. Romantic love, on the other hand, is the natural byproduct of committed love. It is the strong emotion, excitement, and passion generated when you genuinely *respond* to each other. Like the rushing waters that carve out a river bed, romantic love deepens the path of love already there.

Have you ever observed that women seem more interested in romance than men? Dr. James Dobson reveals why women have this inclination:

> For a man, romantic experiences with his wife are warm and enjoyable and memorable—but not necessary. For a woman, they are her lifeblood. Her confidence, her sexual response, and her zest for living are often directly related to those tender moments when she feels deeply loved and appreciated by her man.[7]

While men are not as oriented to romance, I encourage both men and women to recognize the value of developing this aspect of marriage.

Encouraging Romance

I have four practical suggestions to help you foster romantic love within your marriage. Couples, if you want to generate some heat, you've got to light a fire! That means that you must concentrate on the issues below.

First, *find or relearn each other's love language.* Every person is wired differently, responding individually to events. Successful marriage partners understand this and seek to discover the expressions of love meaningful to each other. If you learn how your spouse best experiences love and then express love to him or her in that way, your spouse will feel highly valued. That expression of value is a key part of romance.

Over the years, I have heard from many couples that "romance" means different things to different people. One husband told me, "Romance is the unexpected little things that Judy does for me. Sometimes she'll make a special coffee and bring it out to me. Sometimes I have a note in my lunch. Romance for me is the unexpected surprise." One wife told me, "Angus made window boxes for me, and for me, that was very romantic and loving. He won't write a poem for me, but he will use his skill as a carpenter. That's romantic!" Still another wife said, "Romance is feeling truly loved and special. You think, 'He did that just for me.'"

Over our twenty-plus years of marriage, I have written my wife Naomi fifteen or sixteen poems. I asked her recently, "Is a poem romantic for you?" Her answer was a wise one. She said, "I know that you sat down and thought about it. You took your time, chose words and thought about me. That makes me feel especially loved and important, and because of that, a poem is definitely romantic." Notice that she didn't necessarily consider the poem romantic, but she valued as romantic the thought behind it.

Ask yourselves, individually, these questions: Have I learned my spouse's love language? Do I know the things that make him or her feel especially valued? Have I recently expressed that kind of high value? Is our marriage a continuing love affair? Seek to express love to each other in the love language each of you hears best.

Second, couples also deepen romantic love by *creating positive, shared experiences* together. If you ask successful couples to think back to a special time they had together, most of them will readily relate any number of such times. A wife told me this story:

> One of my favorite moments in our marriage was one night when the snow was falling and neither one of us could sleep so we went and sat out on the couch. It was right before some surgery I needed. We talked about our fears, how we were going to cope and for hours watched everything turn white. It was just magical.

Notice that this happened right in their own home. Their shared emotion created a sense of magic. This happened because they set aside time for each other.

Spouses need to take advantage of whatever time they have together. Some couples are in a season of their marriages in which they can take weekly dates. Great! If you're in that season, share those experiences together and make them memorable. An unexpected lunch at Denny's or a special candlelight dinner—either can be romantic if you see them as opportunities for a shared experience. Special times away like an enrichment weekend can also be wonderfully romantic. They deepen your marital bond.

Listen to what one husband so articulately expressed to me recently:

> Whether it's a minute or a weekend, I want to build memories with Jennifer. I want that emotionally. I've gone through Scripture and watched how many times God says, "Build an altar, build a memorial here. Do this here because it will point back to something." I think we need memorials in our lives, too: memories, anchors, that build our relationship.

This husband does everything he can to deepen the emotional bond with his wife through shared experiences.

As you create positive experiences together, remember to allow yourself the pleasure of spontaneity and playfulness. Variety can be just the ticket for spicing up your romance. Plan a rendezvous in the middle of the day. After taking care of the kids, whisk your spouse away to an undisclosed location! Take a late-night, moonlit walk. Laugh together. Write a love letter or poem to your partner. You can do it!

Third, husbands and wives can also *use their imagination* to grow in romantic love. Use the video screen of your mind to remember past experiences of shared romantic love and to anticipate new ones. What we hold in our minds will tend to direct our actions. Spouses who enjoy the romantic element in marriage *think* about each other in certain ways. They use their God-given imaginations to think warm, tender thoughts about their spouses. Marriage expert Dr. Ed Wheat sums it up well:

> So build romantic love on your side of the marriage by thinking about your partner, concentrating on positive experiences and pleasures out of the past, then daydreaming, anticipating future pleasure with your spouse.[8]

Maybe you've come home to your husband or wife at some time and heard him or her say, "I've been thinking about you all day." Perhaps your spouse has then given you a warm, sensual kiss. *That's* the power of imagination!

Finally, *touching and talking* are two important ways to encourage romantic feelings. A wife told me something recently that I've heard many times before: "One of the most romantic things my husband can do is talk to me. A meaningful conversation with him definitely makes me feel romantic." Think back to your courting days. Remember how much you talked together? Remember the feelings of closeness such conversations elicited?

That's why working through this book is a romantic idea! You'll talk about important issues, and those conversations will draw you closer together. As you talk, also remember that the ability to listen to your spouse's heart is also an act of love.

Touching also encourages romantic feelings. I'm talking again about nondemand touching. If you watch intimate couples, you usually see them hold hands, give hugs, sit close together. Most of us feel warmth when someone holds or tenderly touches us. Don't neglect this simple act that can so wonderfully fan the flames of romantic love.

3. Befriending

One final component of married love that deepens the emotional bond between husbands and wives is the element of friendship. Close spouses consistently report that they are each other's best friends. "Best friends" doesn't mean that a husband and wife are enmeshed together in a way that excludes others. It does mean, however, that both partners invest more heavily in their friendship with each other than in any other relationship. They lavish major investments of time and thought and openness on each other, and these investments deepen the bond of friendship.

As you work to enrich your marriage, what can you do to deepen your friendship with each other? The emotional intimacy of friendship begins when couples consciously decide to share their worlds, melding their activities, feelings, and dreams together in shared experience. Partners who feel distance in their relationship often do so because they gradually begin to experience different worlds. Perhaps one spouse spends larger amounts of time at work; perhaps the other has gradually learned to invest in other interests. Husband and wife talk less and less. They do fewer activities together.

The key concept in deepening your friendship as a couple is the issue of *sharing*. If you want to develop a deeper friendship with your spouse, share yourself in a variety of ways. If you share the same world with each other, you'll develop a satisfying friendship.

Of course, all of this takes time. Sometimes we think that we'll get by with "quality time." That term has a nice ring to it, but it just won't wash. Like panning for gold, quality time is sifted from the earth of quantity time. If you truly want to share with each other, you must commit your most precious commodity to each other: time.

Share Activities and Interests

You can share with each other in a variety of ways. First, you can develop your friendship by sharing varied activities. Do things together! Choose activities as mundane as accompanying each other to the grocery store or as exotic as a Caribbean cruise, and include everything in between. "Togetherness" is the norm for best friends.

This togetherness means intentionally *looking* for ways to share interests and hobbies. A few years ago, Naomi and I wanted to find a way to develop a shared interest. Since we have always loved watercolor paintings, we decided to take a watercolor painting class together. I took a long lunch every Wednesday for five weeks to attend this class with Naomi. While we enjoyed the subject matter, we truly valued the time together sharing the experience. And after the class ended, we spent some wonderful time together enjoying this new hobby.

Some friends of mine bought a canoe recently, and they

spend many warm summer evenings paddling around together. The husband gets in from work, and husband and wife then take the canoe to a local lake and spend a few hours together talking and enjoying the scenery. Through this hobby they've deepened and renewed their friendship. The last time I saw them, they were still talking about how much they enjoyed their time together.

Many couples deepen their friendships by sharing projects together. Over the years, Naomi and I have enjoyed putting up wallpaper, planting gardens, decorating the house—you name it. These and many other projects have deepened our partnership and created great memories.

Partners interested in deepening their friendship must actively look for ways to share activities and interests. Take a moment right now to evaluate whether you have sufficient shared activities and interests to develop your couple friendship. If you think you could use a boost, brainstorm some common interests and ways to develop your friendship through those interests. Then pick one idea to pursue.

Share Thoughts and Ideas

In addition, best friends not only do things together, they share thoughts and ideas. They talk freely on a variety of levels. They offer opinions that stimulate discussion.

Proverbs 27:17 gives us a great word picture of friendship: "As iron sharpens iron, friend shapes friend" (Knox). Used as a comparison to friendship, the image of iron sharpening iron conveys a healthy clash of personalities and views. Real friends develop and mold each other's character. They do this by being vulnerable, sharing their ideas, thoughts, and responses to life's events. Through this exchange, both partners change and grow. As a result, such friends develop a deepening respect for each other and a growing relationship between them.

When was the last time each of you discussed your opinion about a political candidate or shared how you were applying a certain Scripture in your life? How about that talk you need to have concerning your children? If you keep your conversations confidential and commit to accepting each other even when you disagree, sharing thoughts and ideas will be an exhilarating adventure of growing closer.

Share Your Emotions

And finally, one last element of close friendship is the ability to share your emotions with each other. Remember back to your days of courting? Remember how you could share with each other your deepest emotions, knowing the other would understand? Remember how this sharing and understanding created a bond between you?

Partners who want to grow in their friendship must continue to share their inner feelings. In Chapter 5, I discussed the value of self-disclosure to deepening intimacy. Communicating emotions is one of the deepest levels of such self-disclosure. And when one of you discloses, the other needs to listen. If your partner is your best friend, you'll want to listen when he or she shares joy or excitement. You'll listen when he or she needs to share hurt or pain. The sharing of emotions, positive or negative, helps create emotional attachment to each other. That's why I suggest the "check-in" in Chapter 5. You need a plan for staying aware of each other's emotional state.

Are you beginning to see how interconnected these components are? You develop a deepening emotional attachment as you learn to express caring, romance, and friendship. Now choose one of the exercises below and begin to work on these vital areas of your marriage. Or do all three exercises if you have the time and inclination.

Exercise 1: Caring Behaviors

One way to increase your emotional attachment to each other is to communicate about caring behaviors. Many times you can enrich your marriage by making small changes. This exercise will help you pinpoint some small changes that would communicate caring to each other.

Ask each other the following question,[9] and listen to each other's response (each of you may want to write a few answers on paper before you talk, or you might simply talk through the question as you go): "What would you like me to do for you that would really demonstrate how much I care?"

Answers to this question must be measurable, specific, and positive. Don't say, for example, "Stop being so insensitive." Make specific, positive requests such as "It would mean a lot to me if you would give me a kiss when you first come in from work and then spend five minutes telling me about your day."

Think for a moment about the small, caring behaviors that would increase the "warm fuzzies" between you. These behaviors might vary from calling your spouse during the day to talk for a moment to finding a time to pray with your spouse during the week. Avoid chores if possible.

Exercise 2: Rekindling Romance

Now's a good time to bring out your champagne glasses and sparkling cider. Set out the cheese, crackers, and chocolate mints. Light the votive candle you brought along. Pull out the CD or cassette player, and play your favorite music.

Now that you're comfortable and relaxed, talk through the following questions. You may want to write your responses down individually before sharing with each other. Or you might choose to plunge right ahead. Do what suits you best.

1. What acts of affection really make me feel close to you?

2. How have you praised or complimented me recently that I especially enjoyed?

3. In *my* love language, what specific actions and words are most romantic to me?

4. In the next several months, how can we schedule dates together that we will both enjoy?

5. What can we do to lighten up our marriage and bring more humor and laughter into the relationship?

6. As we look to this coming year, how can we make sure that romance is a part of our relationship?

Now finish this conversation by sharing three qualities that you admire or appreciate in each other. Use this opportunity to affirm each other!

Exercise 3: Our Friendship

Deepening your friendship usually involves talking about your present relationship and making some decisions about the future. Use the questions below to have a conversation about this issue. Either write down your answers ahead of time and take turns sharing or simply talk through the questions as you go.

1. Are we deliberately sharing the same world—our time, interests, feelings, thoughts, goals, and ideals? Why or why not?

2. What are some activities and interests that we share together that I really enjoy?

3. What new activities could we pursue to build our friendship?

4. Do we regularly share our ideas, thoughts, and emotions? If not, how could we help each other in this area?

5. How can we structure our lifestyle so we can share more of our world together?

Now turn to Appendix B, "Our Commitment to Marriage Enrichment" (page 184) and, in the space provided, jot down insights you've gained from this chapter and changes you could make to further enrich your marriage.

CHAPTER NINE

Handling the Hot Spots

I'll never forget what happened many years ago when I was in seminary. During that time, my wife ran a day care in our home. I often studied in a room next to the kids' play area, and one day I overheard an interesting interaction. A little girl had somehow roped a seven-year-old boy into playing house with her. He obviously wasn't enthusiastic, but he couldn't get out of it. After playing for a while, the boy and girl began to argue. I could hear this young boy getting more and more frustrated. Just as I peeked around the corner to see what was happening, this seven-year-old boy stood up, put his little fists on his hips, and yelled at his female playmate, "If I had known it was going to be this way, I never would have married you!"

Naomi and I have laughed many times over that incident so many years ago. Of course, the boy's words strike a serious chord. I don't know where the boy had heard those words spoken. Regretfully, spouses sometimes do speak such words to each other. They become frustrated over an issue or a continuing problem, and they don't know what to do about it. Instead of handling the problem, they succumb to their frustration.

In contrast to such reactions, successful couples handle problems before they cause a deep rift. A study done in the eighties with over seven hundred husbands and wives found that couples who discussed martial differences, while sometimes uncomfortable during the process, had fewer subsequent problems in their relationships.[1] Successful couples handle problems, and they do it primarily by talking through each difficulty. They may experience a bit more stress during times of conflict resolution, but those couples experience far *less* stress in the long run because they choose to communicate.

Some time ago, I sat with a couple who had enjoyed a good marriage for many years. As we talked, this husband told me, "We don't usually fight. But if we do, it's either about sex or money." I call these and other such areas of conflict "hot spots." Handling the hot spots is a part of keeping your marriage alive and well. In this chapter, I'd like to offer you an open door of discussion for the two hot spots which that husband mentioned—sexuality and finances—because so many couples struggle with those two issues. This chapter is not a comprehensive approach to each subject but a selective one designed to stimulate your thinking and discussion.

Throughout this book, I've tried to give a positive and practical approach designed to deepen your existing marital bonds. This chapter is designed as an optional foray into the specifics of two common problems should you need it. If you think you're doing well in these two areas, great! If you believe a discussion of these topics would benefit you, please proceed.

The Sexual Relationship

Secular literature indicates that many married couples experience difficulty in the sexual aspect of their relationships. Certainly, my informal surveys with Christian couples indicate to me that Christian couples experience many of the same problems. Believers can't take this area for granted. Most spouses must spend time together discussing this part of their relationship if they want to experience satisfaction in it. As partners openly talk about their sex life, they can overcome most of the difficulties they experience.

A mutually satisfying sexual relationship significantly enhances a marriage relationship. The good news is that most Christian experts in the field of sexuality, including Dr. Cliff Penner and Dr. Ed Wheat, agree on one significant truth: Any Christian couple can have a satisfying sex life. In a recent interview, clinician and author Dr. Cliff Penner was asked what percentage of couples can attain a satisfying sex life. His reply? "One hundred percent of them."[2] Dr. Ed Wheat, an expert in this field, agrees: "The promise of sexual fulfillment is available to any husband and wife who will choose to enter into God's plan for their marriage."[3] That's right! Every couple can find satisfaction in the sexual relationship. The information that follows offers several keys for sexual satisfaction.

The Biblical Ideal

A biblical understanding of sex is important for Christians who want a satisfying sex life. Hebrews 13:4 says, "Marriage should be honored by all, and the marriage bed kept pure." The "marriage bed" directly refers to a couple's sexual relationship. This passage emphasizes the honor given to this part of a couple's married life.

First Corinthians 7:3 also emphasizes God's will for a married couple's sexual relationship: "The husband should fulfill his marital duty to his wife, and likewise the wife to her husband." The verses that follow in this passage explain that spouses' bodies belong to each other and spouses should not withhold their sexual selves from each other but give themselves freely. This First Corinthians passage clearly emphasizes the need for a regular sex life, one that centers on the mutual needs of both partners.

As well, Genesis indicates that God created us as males and females—we are sexual beings by nature. The Genesis 2 account of Adam and Eve's "one flesh" relationship (verse 24) includes the aspect of their sexuality.

Actually, God has dedicated an entire book of the Bible to amorous love. Song of Songs depicts the excitement of two lovers' sensual journey, describing the pleasure they take in each other.

Finally, one of the most straightforward passages about the sexual relationship is found in the book of Proverbs: "Rejoice in the wife of your youth. A loving doe, a graceful deer—may her breasts satisfy you always, may you ever be captivated by her love" (5:18–19). "Captivated" means exhilarated or intoxicated, the emotional thrill associated with the sexual adventure! Such words affirm that sexuality is God's gift. We must receive and enjoy it as a gift from Him.

The bottom line is this: The Bible affirms sex within the context of married love.

Satisfying Sex Is a Relationship Issue

Listen to writer Mike Mason's observation: "What the sex life really demands is the loving gift of the self, the sincere devotion of the whole heart."[4] Mason understands the importance of the whole relationship to sexual satisfaction. Authors Ed and Gaye Wheat concur: "A couple cannot separate sex from the rest of the marriage....everything that happens in the marriage has its effect upon the lovemaking experience."[5] Even secular specialists list interpersonal problems such as partner rejection, marital discord, and failure to communicate as some of the most serious elements of sexual dysfunction.[6] The level of a couple's satisfaction with their sex life depends on the context of their entire relationship.

We can make a few implications from this idea, one being that unselfish love ultimately leads to a satisfying sexual relationship. When you lovingly care for each other in any number of ways, when you both place a priority on the relationship as a whole, you'll tend to experience satisfaction and fulfillment in your sexual relationship. With that in mind, follow the practical suggestions below; they will help you think through what Mason calls the "devotion of the whole heart."

Communicate Directly

To enhance your sexual relationship, you will benefit from *direct communication about your sex life.* Spouses who talk about their sex life tend to experience greater satisfaction. And yet Christian psychologist Alan Loy McGinnis reveals a startling fact about couples' communication regarding sex:

> One of the last barriers to come down as two people become more and more intimate is the wall of secrecy around their sexual feelings. One of the amazing discoveries I've made in my work is that a majority of married couples never discuss the topic of sex! They have done it regularly for 25 years, but they've never talked about it. Often they do not even have the vocabulary for doing so.[7]

I agree with McGinnis that a couple's sex life is one of the most difficult topics to discuss. Such discussion can elicit pride, insecurity, and even embarrassment.

Tom and Gina confirm McGinnis's claim. These two had a good marriage. They loved each other and were thoroughly committed to their marriage. In fact, they were good friends. But Tom tended to be somewhat passive, and Gina was shy by nature. So while their sexual experience together had disappointed both of them for fourteen years, they had *never* had a prolonged discussion on the issue. Gina thought that Tom should know what she needed and that if she communicated about their lovemaking, the sex act would become mechanical. But their lack of communication led to misunderstandings. Fortunately, Tom and Gina eventually overcame their embarrassment and insecurity, and they learned to talk to each other. As they did, they found greater satisfaction and enjoyment in their sexual relationship.

Couples must bring down the "wall of secrecy" in this area of their marriages. Spouses must communicate their feelings and their sexual needs. In my experience, men have more difficulty with this than women. A man's unwillingness to discuss the issue often begins early in the marriage. One young man told me this: "When we got married, I thought we would have sex four or five times a week. When I approached her, she wasn't responding that often. I felt rejected. I didn't know what to do." Had he talked to his wife about it? Unfortunately not. Another man, married twenty years, told me, "It just seems that as a Christian husband, *my* desires shouldn't matter. No matter how much I try though, I can't seem to overcome some of the feelings that are there. When some of my needs aren't met, I have to work at not feeling angry about it." Had this husband talked to his wife about his feelings? Unfortunately not.

How do you speak to your spouse about this topic? Just as you would any other issue—you deliberately set out to have a conversation about it. You sit down and say, "Honey, I'd like to talk to you about something that's important to me." You choose to bring down the "wall of secrecy" and reveal who you are and what you are feeling. The young man I mentioned above needed to say, "Sometimes when you don't want to have sex, I feel rejected. Can we talk about it?" You acknowledge that your feelings are important, that your needs can be communicated. These kinds of discussions, while uncomfortable or tense at the time, bring couples closer together.

Sex therapists Cliff and Joyce Penner offer this advice:

> Communicate with your husband or wife. Set aside a special time for this sharing—a time each of you knows is designated for talking about your sexual activity. Often they (couples) think, *If I am that blunt about what I would like, it'll take all the fun, spontaneity, and mystery out of it*.... Keeping secrets from your spouse about what you desire is a *barrier* to sexual fulfillment.... The more you know about yourself and about what you desire, and the more you communicate those wishes to your partner without placing demands on him or her, the more enhancement you can expect.[8]

Sometimes couples say, "I don't want to hurt my spouse." I understand. Naturally, you need to filter everything you say through love. However, if communication about your sex life leads to a closer relationship, your discussion will be an act of love.

In addition to communicating *about* your lovemaking, you may benefit from communicating *during* and *after* your lovemaking. Couples who communicate while making love find their satisfaction level increase. What would a husband or wife say at such a time? You can speak endearments and words of love. The Song of Songs illustrates such communication. Solomon says of his bride, "How beautiful you are, my darling! Oh, how beautiful!" (Song of Songs 4:1). He then allows his eyes to drink in her physical form: "Your graceful legs are like jewels.... Your breasts are like two fawns" (Song of Songs 7:1,3). Such sexual affirmation enriches a lovemaking experience.

Later, you might communicate about how you can please

each other even more. And don't forget to affirm each other for the ways you brought satisfaction to each other. Experts Cliff and Joyce Penner say, "The process of affirming can be the most valuable, beautiful part of the total sexual experience. It can be a time of tenderness, of closeness, of having shared something extremely intimate and personal."[9] Hearing that you have brought pleasure and satisfaction to your spouse is wonderfully affirming to the whole experience.

I encourage you to take advantage of the exercise at the end of this chapter to communicate about this important aspect of your marriage.

Recognize Your Differences

To have a satisfying sexual relationship, you must also *recognize how differently husbands and wives view the sexual experience.* A woman views her sexual experience in terms of the total relationship. She wants to feel loved and cherished as a person. When her husband sensitively responds to her emotional and spiritual needs, she is more sexually responsive. A woman wants what has been called "all day lovemaking," a feeling that her husband has loved her in various ways all day long. For a man, however, sex is much more physiological. A man is quickly aroused and quickly satisfied. Because he's so physiologically driven regarding sex, he may want intercourse with his wife ten minutes after they have had an argument. She, on the other hand, probably won't.

Dr. James Dobson says that the way a wife "feels about her husband sexually is a by-product of their romantic relationship at that time. If she feels close to him...loved by him...protected by him...then she is more likely to desire him physically."[10] Dobson is right. For that reason, improving a couple's sexual relationship often revolves around a man's willingness to change. Husbands, are you willing to be attentive to your wife, helping her feel loved? Are you willing to progress slowly during intercourse, allowing your wife to guide your advances? Are you willing to focus on *her* needs? A husband's willingness to change in these ways can make all the difference in enhancing a couple's sexual relationship.

Having said that, a man benefits from his wife's sensitivity to his needs as well. I have come to the conclusion that what a man wants most in this area is for his wife to be sexually responsive. He wants to know that his wife is interested in sex. When she isn't, he feels rejected. But when his wife has a positive attitude about sex, he finds it much easier to sexually pursue her in the best way for her.

Further, *husbands must remain flexible because a woman's sexual desires and responses change from one time to the next.* Husbands have said to me, "I just can't understand my wife. One time she responds to me one way, another time she doesn't like what I'm doing. I'm confused!" Men must remember that women have complicated physiological systems including hormonal changes and a monthly cycle. Men are much more stable in their sexual responses. What's the implication? Men, don't assume that a step-by-step approach to sex will work every time. You'll have to listen to your wife to know what will satisfy her during each sexual experience.

Anticipate Development

Spouses should *anticipate growth in their sexual relationship.* Interview successful couples who have been married thirty or forty years, and they'll tell you this: The sexual aspect of their relationship has developed over the years. Sex can continue to be exciting throughout marriage. Why? Because partners continue to grow in their ability to please each other. Sexual desire may diminish somewhat at times in marriage, but the ability to have wonderfully satisfying sexual experiences together does not.

A Good Book Will Help

Finally, you might want to read a book dedicated to sexual fulfillment within marriage. It is true that some couples experience sexual dissatisfaction because they lack specific knowledge. For example, lack of knowledge about how males and females experience arousal and orgasm would surely hinder a couple's sex life. Both partners must know how the male and female bodies work sexually.

If you haven't read at least one good book in this area, I know you will greatly benefit from exposure to the basics. Cliff and Joyce Penner's books *The Gift of Sex* or *Restoring the Pleasure* are both helpful. Dr. Ed Wheat's book, *Intended for Pleasure,* is a classic. Certainly, you could find other good books as well. If you need greater understanding of the various aspects of your physical relationship, such books can clear up many misunderstandings that may hinder your sex life.

If your sexual relationship is a hot spot for you, education could be part of the solution. Also do the exercise at the end of this chapter; it can help you identify ways to improve your sex life.

Finances

Rich and Heather got married in the seventies. Both of them were believers, were excited about their new marriage, and looked forward to a bright future. Rich had just graduated from college and landed an entry-level job in business. His monthly take-home pay was considerably below a thousand dollars. Heather had only a part-time job.

Rich and Heather bought a small home and did what many new couples did at that time: They bought furniture with a credit card. A year later, they had a baby and decided that Heather would stay home to care for their new baby boy. As time went by, they found it easier and easier to borrow on credit.

After six years, they had a five thousand dollar credit card debt. And about that time, the lending rate shot up to 16 percent. Their debt became harder and harder to handle.

Along the way, Rich and Heather made other mistakes. Since money was tight, they avoided talking about it. Instead of taking a hard look at their financial status, they found it easier to ignore the growing debt. However, as the debt mounted, so did the pressure. Soon, they were fighting about money, finding it hard not to blame each other. After ten years of marriage, their financial situation was their number one hot spot.

Four Important Decisions

If you need to handle this hot spot, you can make four decisions that will help you deal with finances in a positive way. Each of these decisions will require a number of discussions. You'll have to talk and talk again. The exercise at the end of this chapter is designed to help you begin the discussion. For now, see if the decisions below make sense to you.

First decision: Eliminate your credit cards. The credit trap is perhaps the number one reason for financial pressure in marriage. Most of us receive scores of preapproved credit cards in the mail every year. Gaining credit is the easiest thing in the world, and many couples find it too hard to resist. Recently, my family stopped for hamburgers at Burger King, and the cashier offered us the choice of paying with our VISA card. When you can charge your hamburger and fries, something is wrong!

While Scripture does not absolutely forbid credit, it certainly makes a case against it. "The borrower is servant to the lender," says Proverbs 22:7. If you've been in debt, you know the truth of this proverb. And financial slavery does nothing but add pressure to married life.

Can you live without a set of credit cards? Absolutely. For the first ten years of our marriage, Naomi and I did not own a credit card. Instead, we saved for items that we needed, then paid cash for them. Sometimes we found this hard; it meant waiting for things we needed. But this system saved us the crushing burden that consumer debt places on a marriage. When our financial resources increased, we used a credit card for convenience, paying it off every month so we didn't have to pay the interest.

Deciding as a couple to avoid the credit card trap may be one of the best things you can do for your marriage.

Second decision: Establish a budget. A budget will help you avoid the trap of consumer debt and the pressure it brings. It will eliminate guesswork. In order to make such a spending plan, sit down and communicate about your financial resources and how to allocate them. Many tools on the market today aim at helping couples make a budget. Christian author Larry Burkett has written numerous excellent books on the subject. If you don't have a budget, Burkett's books will offer much practical advice.

Aside from the obvious advantage of helping you manage your money and live within your means, a budget has another benefit to your relationship. Even without a budget, someone still has to control the checkbook. Let's say a wife is in charge of keeping track of the finances. Her husband comes to her and asks, "Can we afford a new pitching wedge for me?" Now she's in a real dilemma. If she says "no," she's an ogre; if she says "yes," she may blow that month's spending. Perhaps you've been caught in such a quandary. What does she do? You can see the potential for conflict.

When a couple establishes a budget, something far different happens. Let's say this husband comes with the question, "Can we afford a new pitching wedge for me?" How does the wife respond? "Let's look at our budget and see how much is left in our entertainment category or in our miscellaneous category."

They both examine the budget that they've agreed on previously to see if they have the money. This couple avoids a potential conflict.

The key is that both husband and wife must agree on a budget. It doesn't matter who writes the budget; what's important is that both husband and wife examine the budget, fine-tune it, agree on it, then live by it. This obviously requires a good deal of conversation in the drafting of such a plan and in its administration. Both partners must be involved, regardless of who pays the bills every month. Unless a couple talks about their finances and makes decisions together, this area will continue to be a hot spot.

Third decision: Establish a tithe. All Christian couples will want to give 10 percent of their income to God. When Naomi and I were married in 1975, we talked about how we would honor God in our finances. We knew that everything we had belonged to God and that He expected us to manage His money in a way that would bring Him glory. We decided that we would establish tithing in our family. We decided that this would never change, regardless of our financial situation.

Was this decision ever challenged? Of course. Any time you make a commitment based on principle, some situation will come along to test your resolve. When I attended seminary, we faced some financial difficulties. We might have been tempted to discontinue our tithe, but frankly, we never considered that option. We believed our tithe belonged to God. For every dollar that came in, a dime went to God. I can say that in twenty-plus years of marriage, God has never failed to care for us financially. God has honored our decision to tithe, blessing us financially year after year.

I know He will do the same for you if you commit to tithing faithfully.

Fourth decision: Pray together about your finances. This is such an important act. When spouses take their financial concerns to God, they join together in unity. The pressures tend to drop away because they commit their needs to the Lord. Couples who pray together find that God meets them in unique ways.

In our first year of marriage, I was an English teacher at a high school. My first-year's contract was for $8,900. This meant that I had a take-home pay of about six hundred dollars a month. Naomi was finishing college, and we had to pay for her schooling each quarter. We didn't have much room for error in our budget, believe me!

At the end of my first year of teaching, I had to go to summer school. Naomi still had a year left at the University of Washington. As we looked at our finances, it seemed clear that our income couldn't possibly pay for her schooling and mine. What were we going to do? Our tithe would have just about covered Naomi's tuition. But we did not consider that as an option. Instead, we trusted that God would provide in a different way.

One day we were reading the Scriptures together and came across Romans 4. This chapter describes Abraham's faith. As we read, these words stood out to us: "Yet he did not waver through unbelief regarding the promise of God, but was strengthened in his faith and gave glory to God, being fully persuaded that God had power to do what he had promised" (Romans 4:20–21). As we read this passage, God spoke to each of us simultaneously about how to apply it. We decided that our need for Naomi's tuition was something that God wanted to provide for us. But instead of asking for this tuition, we began to thank Him for it ahead of time. Every day as we prayed together, we would give glory to God: "Thank you, Father, that you care about us. Thank you that this tuition money is being provided for us."

Some would say that we were being presumptuous. Frankly, we have not been led to pray so boldly very many times in our marriage. But I believe that God wanted to teach us a lesson through this situation.

As the summer approached, Naomi and I wondered how God would provide. One day I was eating lunch in the faculty lounge around noontime when I got a phone call. I couldn't imagine who would call me in the middle of the day. It was Naomi with news that just couldn't wait. She told me that without her knowledge, her professors at the University of Washington had submitted her name for a scholarship. At a department luncheon that day they had awarded her a full-year's scholarship for her final year of college! Our need had been met!

Seldom has God provided for us so dramatically, but I will tell you this: God has always provided. Praying together about our finances has been such a relief valve for us over the years. I encourage you to commit to praying together about your finances. As you do, you'll see God meet your needs in amazing ways!

Sexuality and finances are two of the hot spots in many marriages. If one or both of these areas are hot spots for you, I encourage you to do each exercise below that corresponds to the issue you need to address.

Exercise 1: Communicating About Sexual Intimacy

Your ability to discuss your sexual relationship is one of the most important factors in developing a satisfying sex life. This exercise will help you share your thoughts and feelings about your sexual relationship.

Remember that sexuality can be a difficult topic for both of you. Be careful to listen and give each other plenty of time to process your thoughts. You may wish to use active listening (see Chapter 5) to help insure that you understand each other.

Use the agree-disagree statements below to begin a discussion. After each of you has stated your opinion, discuss the statement in more depth. The idea is to talk about issues that you might not normally discuss and to gain greater understanding of each other along the way.

1. Sex is a gift from God and should be enjoyed by Christian couples.
Strongly disagree Disagree Agree Strongly Agree

2. We communicate well about our sex life.
Strongly disagree Disagree Agree Strongly Agree

3. Romance is the one thing that I want most in our sexual experience.
Strongly disagree Disagree Agree Strongly Agree

4. I have a positive attitude about our sexual relationship.
Strongly disagree Disagree Agree Strongly Agree

5. I am happy about the frequency with which we have intercourse.
Strongly disagree Disagree Agree Strongly Agree

6. You are sensitive to what I need most in our sexual relationship.
Strongly disagree Disagree Agree Strongly Agree

7. I think variation in position is a good way to add excitement to our sexual experience.
Strongly disagree Disagree Agree Strongly Agree

8. I must have an orgasm every time we have sex in order to feel positive about our sex life.
Strongly disagree Disagree Agree Strongly Agree

9. We have a good understanding of each other's sexual response and know how to help each other achieve a satisfying orgasm.

Strongly disagree   Disagree   Agree   Strongly Agree

10. I feel wanted and needed in our sexual relationship.

Strongly disagree   Disagree   Agree   Strongly Agree

11. Either one of us can initiate sex.

Strongly disagree   Disagree   Agree   Strongly Agree

Now, do either of you need to say anything else about your sexual relationship? Do either of you have any other feelings or thoughts concerning your sex life that you need to communicate? If so, share them now.

Exercise 2: Communicating About Finances

Use the questions below to help you move ahead in the hot spot of finances. If you struggle with this area of your relationship, take special care not to blame each other as you discuss this topic.

1. Have you experienced tension or disagreement in the area of finances over the last six months? If so, what has been the issue?

2. What *feelings* do you have about your financial situation in general?

3. How would you evaluate your effectiveness as a couple in handling money together?

4. What goals do you have about your finances that you haven't reached? How could you do a better job?

5. Look at the decisions suggested in this chapter (eliminate your credit cards; establish a budget; establish a tithe; pray together about your finances). Would any of these decisions

make a positive difference in your financial situation? Which of them are you willing to instigate?

Now turn to Appendix B, "Our Commitment to Marriage Enrichment" (page 184) and, in the space provided, jot down insights you've gained from this chapter and changes you could make to further enrich your marriage.

Part Four

Marriage Enrichment for Life

Chapter Ten

What Now, My Love?

Congratulations! You've done it! You've made time for a weekend away, making a vital investment into the well-being of your marriage. I pray that by completing the material in this book, you've drawn closer to each other, and as a result, the fires of intimacy between you burn more brightly than ever.

The question now is, what's next? During your time away, you probably made some plans and commitments for strengthening your marriage. But once you return home and the responsibilities of home and work overwhelm you, your good intentions can so easily fade into the background. How will you maintain the gains you've made and continue to grow?

My prayer for you is that your weekend together is just the beginning. I hope that you continue to invest time and energy daily into enriching your marriage. For your time away to have maximum impact, you need to follow up with each other. To help you do this, I'd like to offer a few practical ideas that will make this book valuable not just for a weekend but for a lifetime.

Follow Up Your Party for Two!

One of the most important ways to maximize your gains is to plan a specific time, within two or three weeks of arriving home, to assess your weekend. You might plan a Saturday morning breakfast out, an evening after the kids are in bed, or any time that you can talk without interruption.

During your initial follow-up time, discuss two topics. First, take time to share favorite memories from your weekend together. What did God do in your marriage and in your individual lives as you experienced marriage enrichment for a party of two? Did you meet the expectations you discussed in Chapter 3? What surprises enhanced your time together? After sharing memories, affirm any positive changes you've already observed in each other and discuss how those changes have impacted your relationship.

Second, take time to examine Appendix B, "Our Commitment to Marriage Enrichment" at the back of this book (page 184). Review the insights you observed and the changes you thought you should make in your relationship. At this time, form those insights and desired changes into goals that will set a positive direction for the future. (If you weren't able to fill out each section of "Our Commitment to Marriage Enrichment" during your weekend away, simply examine your exercises at the end of each chapter and complete the form at your follow-up meeting.) Write these goals at the end of the form, and commit yourselves to continued growth by agreeing to work on two or three of your goals during the next six to twelve months.

How to Create Goals

As you create your goals, make them *observable* and *positive*. A goal such as "We will share ourselves emotionally" is not specific enough. To make this goal more observable, answer questions such as "*When* will we share?" and "*How* will we share?" Describe what you will actually *do* to promote sharing. For example, you might create an observable goal such as "For the next three months, we will do a 'check-in' with each other at least once a day by asking, 'How are you doing?' or 'How are you feeling?' Each of us must then share not only what we've done but also what we've been feeling for the last few hours."

Goals must be positive as well. Let's suppose that a husband has a habit of jumping in with a solution when his wife shares a problem with him. A goal such as "I will stop providing solutions to my wife's problems unless she asks" is not optimally effective because it only talks about *stopping* a behavior. Instead, concentrate on *beginning* new, positive behaviors; for example, "I will use active listening when my wife shares problems with me, waiting to suggest solutions only when she asks for them."

I know I've offered quite a bit of information in this book, and you could easily feel overwhelmed with the potential to improve various areas of your relationship. I encourage you, instead of trying to work on every potential growth area you've identified, to focus on a few areas that can make a real difference to your relationship. Choose goals to implement in those few areas. When I attend a seminar of any kind—no matter the topic—and I leave with just two or three ideas that I can *actually* implement, I feel great! If you come away from your follow-up time saying, "Here are three ways we'll work to improve our marriage over the long haul," you'll have made great use of your time.

Review Those Goals!

If you want to maximize the benefits of your weekend away and make your follow-up productive, you must review your goals periodically. Without review, your goals will gather dust in some notebook and make no real impact. On the other hand, if you make clear, observable goals then keep them in mind through review, you'll much more likely see real change in your marriage relationship.

How should you review your goals? Any way that makes

sense to you. Tape your goals to your bathroom mirror and read them as you get ready for your day each morning. Review your goals as a couple every Saturday morning during breakfast. Bring along your list of goals on regular date nights and read them aloud together. Talk over your goals at the beginning of each month. It doesn't really matter *when* you choose to review. The key is that you *do* review your goals on a regular basis. Review regularly, and you'll see change.

Finish *A Weekend With the One You Love*

I want to suggest another practical idea for continuing marital growth. It's quite likely that you did not finish all the chapters from this book on your weekend away. If you didn't have a chance to finish, why not take some time in the next few days to complete the chapters you missed? You might wish to plan two or three sessions together over the next month to read the chapters you missed and work through the exercises. As you do this, you might even develop one or two more goals. Add these to your list and remember to review them regularly!

Begin a Marriage Group

Another practical and positive way to continue marriage enrichment is to begin a small group dedicated to marital growth. Find like-minded couples and join together for a biweekly or monthly meeting over the next nine to twelve months. During your first meeting, agree on the goals of the group and how you will run it. Write up a "group covenant" that outlines how your group will operate and give a copy to each couple. Include in this covenant items such as confidentiality, how often you will meet, and what you will study.

I suggest that you find a book or tape series on marriage and agree to work through that resource during your meetings together. Group facilitation could rotate between couples, or one person might be designated for that task. Such a study should include discussion questions and exercises. One excellent series is the Home Builders film series featuring Dennis Rainey. You can purchase this series by contacting Family Life Ministry, Little Rock, Arkansas, 1-800-333-1433. The series offers six forty-five minute videos including "Five Threats to Oneness" and "Resolving Conflict," as well as worksheets to go with them. In addition, Rainey offers less expensive printed materials that cover many of the same topics.

There are also many books stocked at your local bookstore that offer solid help for couples. One excellent tool for marriage groups is Neil Warren's *The Triumphant Marriage,* published by Focus on the Family Publishing. Ten chapters give informative and practical advice for couples of all ages.

One of the couples who field-tested the material in *A Weekend With the One You Love* began a marital-growth group after their weekend away. The group began by working through my first book, *Praying With the One You Love,* because all the couples wanted to foster couple prayer time. The group has helped keep this couple focused on marital enrichment.

Find Marriage Mentors

If you're a young couple—perhaps still in your first five years of marriage—you might benefit by connecting with marriage mentors. A marriage-mentor couple is a "veteran couple"—marriage partners who have successfully developed their marriage relationship and built a solid cache of helpful knowledge and skills. Drs. Les and Leslie Parrott assert that marriage mentoring gives younger couples "a sounding board and a safe place to explore some of their questions about marriage."[1] The Parrotts believe that three meetings with a mentoring couple over a year will provide a valuable avenue of enrichment for any marriage, especially during the first few years.

The best place to look for a mentoring couple is in your home church. Ask your pastor for input; he or she will more than likely be able to suggest a few couples compatible with your personalities and needs. Then choose one of those couples who you feel is right for you. Look for a couple who has been married at least ten years and who evidence a healthy relationship. How will you know if they have a good relationship? Observe how husband and wife treat each other, what they say to and about each other. At church, observe their consistency in reaching out to others and serving God's people. If possible, participate in a Bible class with this couple and listen to the maturity level of both partners' responses.

Once you've decided on a possible couple, approach both husband and wife with the idea of mentoring you and ask them to meet with you to discuss the idea further (you might even invite them over for dinner). During this meeting, tell them what you'd like to gain from a mentoring relationship and ask them to consider meeting with you once a quarter for the next year. If the couple agrees to work with you, then set up an agenda for your quarterly meetings. Make sure you tailor this agenda to your needs as a couple. In your first meeting, you might want to discuss the following question: What are the greatest strengths and the greatest weaknesses in our marriage? If both couples answer this question, you'll have made a great start in getting to know one another.

Visit a Marriage Counselor

I have one more practical idea for moving your marriage in a positive direction: marriage counseling. Don't be alarmed! You don't have to be "in trouble" to consider going to a counselor. Even if you feel good about your marriage, you could still gain many potential benefits from marital counseling. First, a counselor might help your good marriage get better, providing specifics about how you relate to each other and making observations and suggestions not possible otherwise. These specifics might be just the catalyst you need to go even deeper in your relationship.

A marriage counselor may also help you with conflict resolution. Perhaps during your weekend together, some unresolved issues rose to the surface of your relationship. Going to a counselor when you first notice these issues may help head off potentially greater difficulties later on. Taking such a step before problems become overwhelming might make all the difference in keeping your marriage relationship vital and intimate.

If you decide to seek counseling, start by asking your pastor for a referral to a good Christian counselor. Sometimes larger churches will actually have a pastor on staff devoted to counseling and family life. As you choose a counselor, maintain a consumer mentality. Find out the credentials of potential counselors. Ask counselors their backgrounds and their experiences in helping married couples grow closer.

Lifelong Marriage Enrichment

Always remember that marriage enrichment is a process. I often liken the process of marital growth to the adventure of climbing a mountain. Sometimes you make rapid progress in your climb. You feel enthusiastic and ready to move! You experience new vistas and the joy of accomplishment. At other times, you hit plateaus. Your sight is limited, and you're a bit tired. The journey isn't quite as exciting. At still other times, you hit a bit of loose rock and tumble down a few feet. At those times, you pick yourself up and rest for a few minutes. When you're ready, you regain the lost ground and continue on your journey. As you faithfully climb, the peak grows a little closer, urging you to the heights.

Marriage is a lifelong process worthy of our best efforts, requiring an attitude of lifelong marriage enrichment. Couples who understand the importance of being "in process," who are committed to continued growth, find that year after year their marriages improve. What a wonderful adventure! How exciting to grow closer to each other year in and year out, learning to understand each other with greater clarity, to serve with greater joy, to communicate with greater depth. Yes, the "climb" can sometimes produce challenges, but the positive benefits of a successful marriage more than make up for the effort.

As I close this book, this is my prayer for you: May God bless your marital journey with the warmth of His love; may He give you strength for the hard times and grant you joy in the process; may His name be glorified by your example of commitment; and may you enjoy endless hours of marriage enrichment with the one you love!

Appendix A

Getaway Checklist

As you complete your packing, consider taking the following items on your weekend away:

❒ A copy of *A Weekend With the One You Love* (including, if you wish, photocopies of the chapters you intend to cover during your time away)

❒ Paper and pens

❒ Two copies of your wedding vows

❒ Small gifts for each other

❒ Items for a romantic snack time, such as sparkling cider, plastic champagne glasses, cheese, club crackers, chocolates, and a votive candle and holder

❒ CD or cassette player and favorite music

❒ Sporting equipment such as tennis rackets, golf clubs, or bicycles

❒ Books or magazines to read

❒ Planning calendars

❒ Two-person games such as cribbage

❒ Toothbrush, toothpaste, shampoo, and other toiletries

❒ Clothing suitable for your chosen activities and for the weather you'll encounter

APPENDIX B

Our Commitment to Marriage Enrichment

Chapter 4, "Committed Love"

Insights from this session:

Changes needed:

Chapter 5, "Skillful Communication"

Insights from this session:

Changes needed:

Chapter 6, "Effective Conflict Resolution"

Insights from this session:

Changes needed:

Chapter 7, "Vital Spiritual Friendship"

Insights from this session:

Changes needed:

Chapter 8, "Deepening Your Emotional Bond"

Insights from this session:

Changes needed:

Chapter 9, "Handling the Hot Spots"

Insights from this session:

Changes needed:

Chapter 10, "What Now, My Love?"

Goal 1:

Goal 2:

Goal 3:

Goal 4:

Goal 5:

Appendix C

Successful Couples' Top Ten Rules for Handling Conflict Fairly

I recently sat down with a focus group of successfully married couples and asked them this question: "Do you operate on a set of rules when you're having a conflict?" They said, "Sure!" To finish this chapter, I want to share their practical "conflict commandments" with you. You may have heard some of these rules before, but the list makes a good reminder.

1. When conflict begins, active listening is a must.
2. Stick to one topic at a time. If more than one issue comes up, it will confuse the conversation.
3. Allow your spouse time to process if needed.
4. Pick the right time and place to resolve conflict. Starting a conversation about a major issue at bedtime is usually not a good idea.
5. Avoid labels and name-calling. This is never appropriate and almost always derails the process.
6. Keep current—don't let offenses build. Take care of negative feelings as quickly as possible. Don't hold things in.
7. Don't take out your anger on your spouse. If you need to, take a timeout to cool down.
8. Ask God to help. He knows more than both of you!
9. Avoid the words "always," "never," or "forever." These are usually projections of blame and bring up past failures.
10. Be willing to ask for forgiveness if you say or do anything wrong. Humility will keep your communication lines open.

Chapter 2:
"Why a Weekend Away?"

1. Neil Warren, *The Triumphant Marriage* (Colorado Springs: Focus on the Family Publishing, 1995), 89.

2. H. Norman Wright, *The Secrets of a Lasting Marriage* (Ventura: Regal Books, 1995), 133.

3. Mike Mason, *The Mystery of Marriage* (Portland, Oreg.: Multnomah Press, 1985), 101.

4. I am indebted to H. Norman Wright for the basic concept of this exercise that I've adapted from *The Secrets of a Lasting Marriage,* 186-187, for marriage-enrichment weekends and pastoral-counseling situations.

Chapter 3:
"Preparing for Your Weekend Away"

1. Dave Arp and Claudia Arp, *The Ultimate Marriage Builder* (Nashville: Thomas Nelson Publishers, 1994), 10.

Chapter 4:
"Committed Love"

1. Warren, *Triumphant Marriage,* 28.

2. James Dobson, *Love for a Lifetime* (Sisters, Oreg.: Multnomah Books, 1987, 1993), 47, 52.

3. Mason, *Mystery of Marriage,* 97.

4. Ibid., 91.

5. Warren, *Triumphant Marriage,* 34.

6. Paula Rinehart, "Two of a Kind?" *Discipleship Magazine* (July/August 1988): 4-6.

7. Allen P. Ross, *Creation & Blessing* (Grand Rapids: Baker Book House, 1988), 126.

8. Warren, *Triumphant Marriage,* 31.

9. Charles M. Sell, *Intimate Marriage* (Portland, Oreg.: Multnomah Press, 1982), 28.

10. Ed Wheat, *Love Life* (Grand Rapids: Zondervan Publishing House, 1980), 119.

11. Warren, *Triumphant Marriage,* 42.

12. Wright, *Secrets of a Lasting Marriage,* 72.

13. David Mace and Vera Mace, *How to Have a Happy Marriage* (Nashville: Abingdon Press, 1977), 48.

14. I am indebted to Neil Warren for the basic concept of this exercise that I've adapted from *Triumphant Marriage,* 35-38, for marriage-enrichment weekends and pastoral-counseling situations.

15. Mason, *Mystery of Marriage,* 95.

Chapter 5: "Skillful Communication"

1. John Stewart, ed., *Bridges Not Walls* (Reading, Mass.: Addison-Wesley Publishing Company, 1973), 19.

2. John Powell, *Why Am I Afraid to Tell You Who I Am?* (Allen, Tex.: Argus Communications, 1969), 54-62.

3. John Gray, *What Your Mother Couldn't Tell You & Your Father Didn't Know* (New York: HarperCollins, 1994), 164.

4. "The 1990 Virginia Slims Opinion Poll," study conducted by the Roper Organization, Inc., Roper Center, University of Connecticut, Storrs, Conn. 06268.

5. David Carlson, *Counseling and Self-Esteem* (Waco, Tex.: Word Books, 1988), 170-176.

6. H. Norman Wright, *Making Peace With Your Partner* (Dallas: Word Publishing, 1988), 92.

7. Dobson, *Love for a Lifetime,* 59.

Chapter 6:
"Effective Conflict Resolution"

1. Mace and Mace, *How to Have a Happy Marriage,* 20-21.

2. Jack R. Gibb, "Defensive Communication," in *Bridges Not Walls,* ed. John Stewart (Reading, Mass.: Addison-Wesley Publishing Company, 1973), 74.

3. I am indebted to many authors who have shown couples how to avoid blame by focusing on actions and feelings. The SAFE strategy is adapted from Andrew Miller and John Pety's *Marital Expectation Training* (Atlanta: Developmental Training Ministries, 1984).

4. Mace and Mace, *How to Have a Happy Marriage,* 113-115, author's adaptation.

5. Gray, *What Your Mother Couldn't Tell You,* 92.

Chapter 7:
"Vital Spiritual Friendship"

1. Dobson, *Love for a Lifetime,* 50.

2. Wright, *Secrets of a Lasting Marriage,* 154.

3. Art Hunt, *Praying With the One You Love* (Sisters, Oreg.: Multnomah Books, 1996), 13.

4. Paul Stevens, *Marriage Spirituality* (Downers Grove: InterVarsity Press, 1989), 21.

5. Dobson, *Love for a Lifetime,* 47.

6. Wright, *Secrets of a Lasting Marriage,* 149.

7. Hunt, *Praying With the One You Love,* 119.

8. Stevens, *Marriage Spirituality,* 44.

9. I am indebted to Paul Stevens for the basic concept of this exercise that I've adapted from *Marriage Spirituality,* 50-51, for marriage-enrichment weekends and pastoral-counseling situations.

10. I am indebted to Paul Stevens for the basic concept of this exercise that I've adapted from *Marriage Spirituality,* 104, for marriage-enrichment weekends and pastoral-counseling situations.

Chapter 8: "Deepening Your Emotional Bond"

1. Henry Cloud, *Changes that Heal* (Grand Rapids: Zondervan Publishing House, 1990), 46.

2. I am indebted to Stephen Corey for the basic concept of the "Emotional Bank Account" that I've adapted from *The Seven Habits of Highly Effective People* (New York: Simon & Schuster, 1989), 188-189, for marriage-enrichment weekends and pastoral-counseling situations.

3. John Powell, *The Secret of Staying in Love* (Allen, Tex.: Argus Communications, 1974), 44.

4. Ross Campbell, *How to Really Love Your Child* (Wheaton: Victor Books, 1977).

5. Wheat, *Love Life,* 183.

6. Ibid., 87.

7. Dobson, *Love for a Lifetime,* 41-42.

8. Wheat, *Love Life,* 89.

9. Wright, *Secrets of a Lasting Marriage,* 136-137, author's adaptation.

Chapter 9: "Handling the Hot Spots"

1. E. Menaghan, "Marital Stress and Family Transitions: A Panel Analysis," *Journal of Marriage and Family* 45 (1983): 371-86.

2. Warren, *Triumphant Marriage,* 123.

3. Ed Wheat and Gaye Wheat, *Intended for Pleasure* (Old Tappan, N.J.: Fleming H. Revell Company, 1981), 16.

4. Mason, *Mystery of Marriage,* 127.

5. Wheat and Wheat, *Intended for Pleasure,* 25.

6. Helen Singer Kaplan, *The New Sex Therapy* (New York: A Brunner/Mazel Publication published in cooperation with Time Books, 1974), 155-167.

7. Alan Loy McGinnis, *The Friendship Factor* (Minneapolis: Augsburg Publishing House, 1979), 31.

8. Clifford Penner and Joyce Penner, *The Gift of Sex* (Waco, Tex.: Word Books, 1981), 106-107.

9. Ibid., 180.

10. Dobson, *Love for a Lifetime*, 84.

Chapter 10:
"What Now, My Love?"

1. Les Parrott and Leslie Parrott, "Couple to Couple," *Focus on the Family Magazine* (November 1996): 10-11.